PAPER
as Art and Craft

Other Books by the Authors:

Thelma R. Newman:

CONTEMPORARY DECOUPAGE
CREATIVE CANDLEMAKING
PLASTICS AS AN ART FORM
PLASTICS AS DESIGN FORM
WAX AS ART FORM

Jay Hartley Newman and Lee Scott Newman:

PLASTICS FOR THE CRAFTSMAN

PAPER
as Art and Craft

The Complete Book of the History
and Processes of the Paper Arts

THELMA R. NEWMAN
JAY HARTLEY NEWMAN
LEE SCOTT NEWMAN

CROWN PUBLISHERS, INC., NEW YORK

TO Jack Newman

Inquiries should be addressed to Crown Publishers, Inc., 419 Park Avenue South, New York, N.Y. 10016.

Library of Congress Catalog Card Number: 72-96648

Printed in the United States of America
Published simultaneously in Canada by
General Publishing Company Limited

Designed by Ruth Smerechniak

Second Printing, October, 1974

acknowledgments

A complete book such as this owes its existence to countless people who have contributed to paper lore, process, and art. Many individuals, institutions, and companies helped us, and the information and work gathered here could never have been compiled without their generous cooperation.

Ernest R. Schaefer was a veritable mine of information. Our very special thanks go as well to Jane Bearman, Lida Hilton, Golda Lewis, and Nell Znamierowski.

Our appreciation also goes to Jack Robinson of Andrews-Nelson-Whitehead, The Bee Paper Company for a generous supply of Aquabee Papers, the Container Corporation of America, Dennison Manufacturing Company for their unstinting help, Myron Horowitz of Brimful House, and Emily Morgan of Fred Leighton Imports, Ltd. The Union Camp Company was extremely helpful with honeycombed papers. The Museum of Contemporary Crafts was a valuable research center. Our thanks as well to Norm Smith for his consistent photo processing.

The individuals, companies, and institutions listed below were all helpful and encouraging. Our debt to them is great.

Activa Products
Aluminum Company of America
American Crayon Company
American Museum of Natural History
American Paper Institute

The British Museum
Bonnie Cashin of Bonnie Cashin Designs
Cepelia Corporation
Bodil Christensen
Edward Ghossn
Kairalla Agency
Kimberly-Clark Corporation
Donald Lloyd McKinley
The Metropolitan Museum of Art
Marjorie Moore
Multiples Gallery
Museum of Modern Art
Patricia Nimocks
Pace Gallery
The Paper Museum, Institute of Paper Chemistry
Mary Walker Phillips
Betty VanBlaircum of Regal Rugs, Inc.
Technical Papers Corporation
Three Arts Group
Victoria & Albert Museum
Waddell Gallery
Jim Hanko of Weyerhaeuser Company

Last, but never least, is our husband/father, Jack Newman: Quartermaster General.

T.R.N.
J.H.N.
L.S.N.

All photographs are by the authors unless otherwise credited.

preface

Paper as Art and Craft was a very enjoyable book to write because of the broad range and history of paper's potential as an art and craft material. Paper encompasses a spectrum of form from primitive crafts to highly sophisticated art and design. It has a rich and long history of use, and yet new concepts and ideas are still emerging because paper is a part of everyday living.

Paper has been a popular item for centuries and is taken for granted because there has been a ubiquitous profusion of it used in every sector of life. But along with its availability comes a tradition of skills and the value that paper can be worked by anyone. Because it is generally inexpensive and easy to find, people explore with it and are apt to try unusual things. Technical problems are minimal, and paper's potential is great.

Working with paper is a discovery process. The ways in which we can alter the basic form of a flat sheet of paper is the overriding concept of *Paper as Art and Craft*. Technical and design concepts, which are central to all projects, are transferable. For example, when folding paper in straight lines or curves, geometry is ever-present inasmuch as geometrical structures grow out of relationships of folds. These forms have direct applications as containers, domes, lampshades, and kites, to name a few.

The focus is on understanding paper's qualities. From that base paper can be applied to any art or craft area from fine arts in collage and sculpture to craft forms in making flowers, weaving, creating decorative papers, binding a book, and so on.

We hope that the vocabulary of paper's potential and examples of good design will lead to discovery of new designs and will be transferable from one medium to another.

As ever, the parameter of paper's potential is your own creative thought.

Contents

chapter 1

Paper: History and Process

Paper is a paradoxical material. It is transient and yet enduring, delicate and strong. It can be a filter or a barrier. Paper ends up in museums and in trash cans. It decomposes in water and has been made into boat hulls, umbrellas, and raincoats. Paper can be insubstantial and yet is used in permanent buildings for domes and fenestration. It is a temporary material, and books have lasted for 1,500 years. Paper is cheap and expensive, abundantly available and scarce. It is made and consumed by the ton and can be so rare that only a few sheets of handmade *gampi* paper are made in a year.

Paper can be transparent, dense, fire resistant, filter thin, rigid, limp, light, heavy, temporary, weatherproof, and long lasting.

It can become any kind of paper by changing its base material, an aspect in its manufacture, or a chemical additive.

There are almost no limitations to what paper can do and how it can be manipulated. It can be cut, folded, curled, twisted, torn, crushed, shredded, macerated, molded, burned, dissolved, laminated, creped, honeycombed, made transparent, die-scored and diecut.

Paper can become almost anything useful from crocheted hats, padded rugs, lanterns, aprons, disposable clothing, partition screens, cuffs, umbrellas, plates, cups; or play forms such as party decorations, kites, paper balloons, pinwheels, togs; or fantasy forms such as origami and art forms like collage and

Fragments of paper of the Eastern Han period (A.D. 25-220), the most ancient paper known to exist in the world. Courtesy: The British Museum

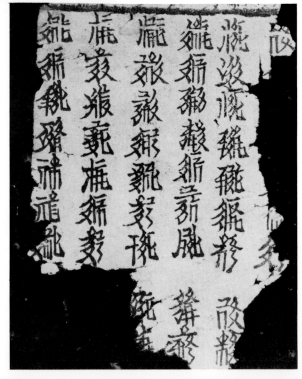

Piece of a manuscript on paper found in 1907 by Sir Aurel Stein in the ruins of the Great Chinese Wall. Circa A.D. 150. Courtesy: The British Museum

sculpture. Paper from its invention has had religious significance, as Chinese funeral garments and money symbols and as Otomi Indian fetish forms and papier-mâché ceremonial masks used in religious processions throughout the world to this day.

The range of paper possibility seems limitless. Paper has been used since its invention in A.D. 105 in countless ways for over 14,000 different products, yet new ways of utilizing paper are still being discovered and will continue to evolve because paper is an expression of everyday living. It is a way and a means of communication.

History of Paper

Early man's expression often was cumbersome: etchings on stones and bones, and paintings or carvings on walls of caves. Men and women searched for quicker, lighter, more portable and easily stored vehicles. People of the Middle East developed beeswaxed boards and palm leaves. The Chinese used silk and clay tablets. Ancient Greeks developed parchment made from animal skins. Four thousand years ago the Egyptians "invented" papyrus, which was a cross-woven mat of reeds pounded into a hard thin sheet. It was not a true paper although it could be written on and rolled into a smaller shape for portability and storage.

Paper, as we know it today, was invented by a Chinese eunuch, Ts'ai Lun, in A.D. 105. It was a thin, felted material formed on flat porous molds from macerated vegetable fibers. Since Mêng T'ien of China invented the camel's hair brush in 250 B.C., writing was revolutionized but required a writing material better than silk and clay. Ts'ai Lun opened the door to a vast realm.

Before the Europeans learned about paper nearly a thousand years later, the Chinese

had invented paper money, an outgrowth of "spirit money" left in graves for the departed. They were the first to use toilet paper and temporary clothing. The Chinese used ornamental paper, some very elaborate such as mandarin coats, to represent various objects. These were burned at funerals.

Dokyo, a Buddhist monk, brought papermaking to Japan in A.D. 610. The Japanese used paper mulberry bark, which became a universal paper base material of the Far East. They further refined the process in numerous small cottage factories, where the handmade paper art and tradition continues today, as well as throughout Asia.

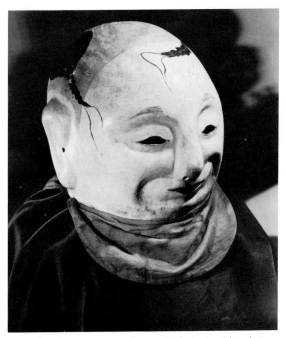

Paper has known universality particularly in old techniques such as papier-mâché, the process used to make this old Tibetan mask. Courtesy: The American Museum of Natural History

The Japanese early found uses for paper in all sectors of their life. This elegant 8-paneled screen, circa 16th century, attributed to Kano Sanraku, is a painting of birds and millet on gold leaf. The screen is made of paper. The size of each screen is 38¾" × 139½". Courtesy: The Metropolitan Museum of Art

A Chinese child's funeral garment that is burned during the child's funeral.

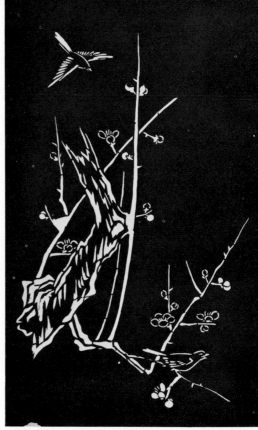

Paper stencils are still used for repeat designs on fabrics. This is a 19th century Japanese stencil. Courtesy: The Metropolitan Museum of Art, Gift of Leon Dabo

A papier-mâché mask used in a Chinese New Year celebration of the Year of the Dragon.

The Muslims uncovered the secret of papermaking when they captured a Chinese paper mill at Samarkand in A.D. 751 and forced Chinese prisoners to teach them the process. Whereas the Chinese and Japanese used mulberry bark, the Arabs employed linen rags in papermaking. Ironically, it was 1,000 years before the papermaking process was introduced to Europe via Xativa, Spain, in A.D. 1151 and another 700 years before the use of wood bark was rediscovered by the Europeans.

From Spain, paper mills spread throughout Europe to Fabriano (1268), Bologna (1282), Cologne (1320), Nuremberg (1390), and to America through the Spaniards to Culhuacán, Mexico, in 1580.

In Mexico, the Mayans had used a kind of paper made from fig tree bark since A.D. 500 and the Aztecs later improved it. Bark paper similar to the Mayans' was made in the South Sea Islands where it was called *tapa*. The Mayans also invented a hard-covered accordionlike book made of this paper called a *codex*. Some of these Mayan and Aztec manuscripts still exist even though the Spanish missionary Diego de Landa burned the library of the Mayans. The Aztecs also used paper as tribute. Mayan priests and dignitaries wore paper costumes and ornaments in sacral dancing. These adornments included crowns, stoles, flags, bracelets, decorations, fanlike head ornaments, and giant banners—all made of *amatyl*.

Paper was brought to Germantown, Pennsylvania, by William Rittenhouse and William Bradford in 1690. There the European tradition of using rags to make paper persisted even though rags were becoming exceedingly scarce. During the Revolutionary War, any scraps of paper were used for messages. People "starved" for paper. Soldiers tore up old books to make wadding for their guns. Women were urged to conserve and collect rags. The shortage continued. In 1855, there is a record of a manufacturer importing Egyptian mummies in order to use the linen fibers and wrappings in papermaking. Yet the use of wood as the base for paper had been known by the Mayans and

Orientals for centuries. With more literate people and a greater demand for the diffusion of knowledge, the supply of linen and cotton rags (and the slow hand process) did not keep up with the demand. The search was on to find a substitute for linen and cotton rags and a faster way to produce paper.

Even though in 1719 a Frenchman, René-Antoine Ferchault de Réaumur, observed wasps using bits of wood to make their paper nests, it was not until 1850 that a German, Friedrich Gottlob Keller, developed a machine for grinding wood into fibers. Problems still persisted. In 1865, the rest of the wood production difficulties were solved when an American, Benjamin Tilghman, discovered how to dissolve unwanted resins in wood with the sulfite process.

Meanwhile, another aspect of paper scarcity was tackled—how to make paper more quickly. Until the beginning of the 19th century all papermaking was done by hand. In 1798, Nicholas-Louis Robert of France invented and patented a crude paper machine. It never succeeded and was brought to England where it was improved by Bryan Donkin with Henry and Sealy Fourdrinier's financial support and was introduced in 1806. (The papermaking machine to this day is called "the Fourdrinier.")

Bit by bit the papermaking machine was improved until it became the huge mechanism it is today, producing $22,224,000,000 * worth of paper and allied products in the United States alone in 1971.

What Is Paper?

If you look at the torn edge of a piece of paper under magnification, you can see that it is made up of matted hairlike fibers of various lengths. These fibers are cellulose or glucose sugar—polysaccharide. Paper does not taste like sugar because plants string

* 1971 report of the American Paper Institute.

Paper has long been a fine art medium. A collage by Juan Gris made of pasted paper, crayon, and oil paint on canvas. Courtesy: The Museum of Modern Art

Dubuffet used markers on white offset paper which was cut and pasted on kraft paper for his collage called "Personnage," 1971, 13¼" × 8". Courtesy: Pace Gallery, New York

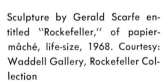

Sculpture by Gerald Scarfe entitled "Rockefeller," of papier-mâché, life-size, 1968. Courtesy: Waddell Gallery, Rockefeller Collection

Kashmiri papier-mâché eggs (India) are purely decorative. Egg shapes, however, have long been a favorite shape of craftsmen. *Courtesy: Brimful House*

together molecules of glucose into chains forming cellulose. Cellulose * is the major component of plant tissues and fibers. It is in plant leaves and stems and in the long fibers in wood. Cotton, for instance, is 90 percent cellulose. These cellulose fibers are bunches of cellulose chains seemingly welded together.

Most paper today is made of wood that has been finely pulverized, bleached, cleaned, and processed chemically to eliminate noncellulose components. The result of this process is the pulp, which is a suspension of cellulose in additives such as binders and water. A great deal of water is used in the process.

To make a ton of paper, 100 tons of water are needed. The wet pulp is deposited on a fine screen until the desired thickness is built up. Most of the water drains off through the screen, more is squeezed out between felts, and what remains is dried with heat, and the whole is pressed with rollers.

What Is True Paper?

According to Dard Hunter, for a material to be classed as true paper, the thin sheets must be made of fiber macerated into individual filaments, intermixed with water, and lifted from the water through sievelike fine screens. When the water drains through the screen holes, a sheet of matted fibers is left on the screen's surface. The basic process has not changed since A.D. 105.

* Special thanks to Ernest R. Schaefer for his help here.

A Cora Indian (Nayarit, Mexico) mask used to celebrate Easter is made of papier-mâché.

Paper cutouts by the Vivanco family in San Andrés Huixcolotla stem from a religious tradition that dates back several centuries. These thin tissue paper cutouts are used to decorate altars and windows and often are used in multiples to hang from ceilings.

A corner in an Otomi Indian house in Mexico demonstrates the use of paper as a cutout table cover, for paper flowers and as an altar canopy.

This papier-mâché fantasy dragon is blown up with firecrackers during Mexican religious holidays. Courtesy: Fred Leighton's, New York

Paper is even employed as decoration for instruments of torture—these banderillos are for the bull. The puffs and trim are made of many layers of tissue paper.

Mrs. Mary Delany, in the late 18th century, made what she called "paper mosaiks." They were painstakingly intricate paper flowers cut from hand-watercolored paper. Courtesy: The British Museum

Stemming from the legacy of hundreds of Mary Delany's "paper mosaiks," a Victorian art emerged. Three-dimensional paper forms were created from multiples of prints. This is a contemporary version by Maxine Ludden. Courtesy: June Meier of the Cricket Cage

Corrugated fiberboard is the material from which Frank O. Gehry designed his "Easy Edges" furniture collection. This rocker has a suedelike surface and bounce. Courtesy: Kairalla Agency

Paper is for burning as well. We start fires with newspaper. Firecrackers are covered with paper. So is this Nepal incense made of twisted ropes of paper. Courtesy: Brimful House

Paper can be die-cut and molded as in the making of these Replogle globes; an inexpensive product can be mass produced from paper. Courtesy: Replogle Globes

Paper has numerous commercial uses as in this paper surgical apron. Courtesy: Superior Surgical Mfg. Co., Inc.

Papyrus, then, is not a true paper, because it is not formed from macerated fibers but is made of laminated slivers sliced from a stalk. And so-called rice "paper" is a misnomer. It also is not a paper. Rice "paper" is a smooth white material cut spirally from the pith of the *kung-shu* tree (*Tetrapanax papuriferum*) found in the hills of north Formosa. Japanese papers commonly referred to as "rice paper" are made from *kozo*, a long-fiber mulberry relative; *mitsumata* (*edgeworthia papyrifera*), a long-fiber material used to make Japanese vellum; and *gampi*, a wild relative of hemp. (The Japanese also make paper from bamboo.)

Other misconceptions are about parchment and vellum. Parchment is made from the split skins of sheep, and vellum is made of calfskin, goatskin, or lambskin exposed for a long time to lime and then scraped with a rounded knife and rubbed smooth with pumice stone. Since neither parchment nor vellum is tanned they are not true leather either.

Parchment and vellum were used centuries ago for books and documents before paper took over. Monks copied manuscripts on parchment and vellum. The Declaration of Independence is on parchment. Even after the advent of printing in Europe, with wood blocks and movable type, parchment was still considered to be the more permanent material.

Tapa, the paper of the South Sea islands area, although made from paper mulberry, is also not a true paper because fibers are not reduced to individual units. Bundles of sticks are soaked until the outer bark becomes soft leaving the soft inner yellow-white bark. The bark is stripped and laid on grass to dry and bleach. Then it is rolled into coils. The strips are then beaten with a wooden mallet until a 3″ piece becomes 18″–20″. Pieces are overlapped in narrow folds and beaten together to form larger pieces.

Related to *tapa* is *amatyl* (paper) of the Otomi Indians in Mexico. They still use their "paper" for witchcraft and black magic, but their ancestors, the Aztecs and Mayans, used a similar process with *amatyl* or cactus to make paper for their sacred ornaments, clothing, and books. This process comes closer to true paper. Bark is boiled with wood ash and water until some disintegration occurs; the fibers become soft and the sap is removed. Pieces are then laid side by side overlapping in a grid pattern on a rectangular board and pounded with a stone beater or burned-hard corncob until meshed together into a smooth sheet. Then the piece is placed on a board in the sun and peeled off when dry.

The *Codex Mendoza*, one of the tribute books of Montezuma II (1480?–1520), identified 42 centers of papermaking in Mexico. Two of the cities paid a tribute of nearly half a million sheets of paper every year.

It is interesting to note that, even though papyrus is not a true paper, *paper*, *papier*, *papel* come from the Greek and Latin *papuros* and *papyrus*. *Bubloi* was a Greek term used to indicate the inner fiber of the papyrus plant. Writings on papyrus were called *biblos* in Greek and *biblia* in Latin, hence the word "bible."

The original method of macerating material for making paper is shown in these two processes. The illustration is from *China: Its Costume, Arts, Manufactures, etc.,* by M. Breton, London, 1813. Courtesy: The Paper Museum, Institute of Paper Chemistry

Making Handmade Paper

Clean cotton or linen rags that have been allowed to soak in water until fermentation begins are macerated and then beaten until the mass triturates into a pulp. A vatman, holding a two-part screen (with a removable frame around the edge) plunges it vertically into the linen-cotton pulp and then quickly turns it upward and lifts it from the vat horizontally while shaking it at first right to left and then front to back to cross and mat the fibers and to drain off water. As the water drains through the screen, fibers remain on the wires of the mold. The vatman then passes the mold to the coucher, who places the sheet (and mold) in a drainage area. When the wet sheet has solidified enough to develop a luster, the coucher removes the frame, turns the mold over, and deposits the wet sheet on a piece of wool felting. When the pile contains 144 sheets, the layman places the sheets and felts in a "wet" press to extract excess water. After pressing, the weight of the paper is reduced tenfold and the fibers are matted and fitted together by the pressure. The layman then removes the paper from the felts, returns the felts to the coucher, and stacks the papers one on top of another. Since the papers are still damp at this point, they are again subjected to pressure, and more water is squeezed out. After this second pressing the papers are separated and built into a different pile, and more pressure is exerted. An animal sizing is applied to writing paper at this time. Again, after more pressing, "spurs" (bundles) of four or five sheets of paper are taken to the drying room and hung up to dry. Years ago the papers were dried over cowhair ropes that were coated with beeswax. In the Orient the paper was allowed to dry on a frame, a smooth board, or a wall in the sun. In India, paper finishing is accomplished by laboriously rubbing the surface with a smooth stone. Burnishing closed the pores of the sheet making it suitable for writing; in England they used an agate. Later in Europe huge pressing hammers were employed and this gave way to the use of glazing rollers.

The deckle left around the edge of the paper was caused by seepage of a small amount of pulp under the frame. This used to be trimmed away, but with the advent of mechanized papermaking soon became a status symbol. Today some machine processes try to imitate the deckle.

This print is of a watercolor painting of the late 18th century. It shows most of the phases of early Chinese paper-making, except for the first stage of the process seen in the previous photo—maceration of the raw materials to a state of individual fibers.

The second stage seen at the left is dipping a hand mold into a vat which holds the fibers in suspension. As the hand mold is brought up out of the vat, water runs through the sieve, leaving the fibers matted on the bamboo sieve-mold. Shaking the mold mats the fibers evenly.

In the center background, a large amount of water is pressed from the very wet layers of paper. A fourth stage is seen in the right foreground. Remaining moisture is removed from the sheets as a fire burns, heating two stucco walls upon which wet sheets are placed to dry.

The last stage is shown in the right background. Paper is examined and counted. Courtesy: The Paper Museum, Institute of Paper Chemistry

A lone Chinese worker makes paper. Note the bamboo stick used to stir the macerated fibers into an even suspension. A bamboo mold leans on the left and stacks of paper drain on the right. Courtesy: Victoria and Albert Museum

An ancient book made of amatyl (paper) from Mexico. Coda of the Aztecs, *El Pueblo de Sol*.

An Otomi papermaker of San Pablito, Puebla, Mexico, pounds amatyl fibers. Note that newly cut fibers hang on a rope while finished sheets of white paper dry on boards in the sun. Photograph by Bodil Christensen

Fibers are arranged in small squares and rectangles before felting them into a sheet. Note that the fibers are soaking in a bowl. Photograph by Bodil Christensen

Squares of fibers are felted together by pounding with a stone or a fire-hardened corn cob. Photograph by Bodil Christensen

From Sierra La Puebla (Mexico) comes this traditional headdress worn for the dance of "Los Moros" (The Moors). Ornamental paper headdresses similar to this were made in pre-Columbian times and used by the Mayans and Aztecs.

An intaglio picture with occult symbols is being formed on white amatyl with dark brown amatyl fibers. Photograph by Bodil Christensen

Doña Camila peels a dry paper intaglio from a wooden board. Photograph by Bodil Christensen

The wet fibers are matted to the base by pounding with a stone. Photograph by Bodil Christensen

Because these amatyl figures are made of dark paper they represent black magic spirits.

White amatyl symbolizes good. This represents a prayer for the pineapple.

This paper doll represents other spirits related to Otomi Indian life.

This intaglio is made of strips of amatyl inlaid into an amatyl background by pounding. Symbols often represent spirits.

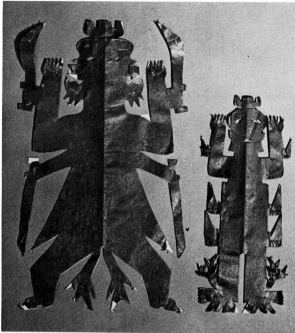

These are paper dolls cut from many colored layers of tissue paper and sewn together at different points. These dolls represent to the Otomi Indians the spirits of the seeds of various crops. They correspond in color and images sprout from sides and top. A doll that represents maguey would be green and have maguey leaves sprouting from the sides.

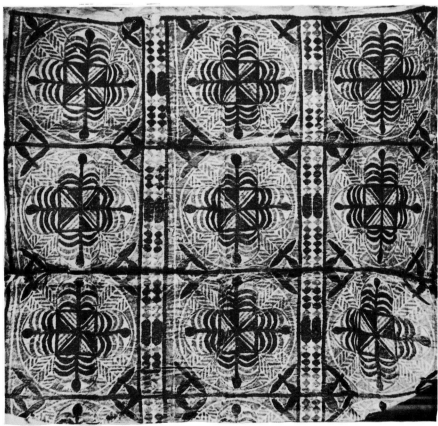

Tapa cloth from the South Sea islands was made by beating the moistened inner bark of the mulberry tree until the narrow strips multiplied in size. This piece was then decorated with berry juices. The colors are various values and intensities of brown. This specimen dates back to the 1930s.

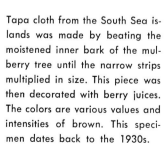

Papyrus, the marsh plant that provided the raw material for papyrus, a paperlike material.

Fibers from Japanese shrubs used in papermaking. *Kozo* is on the left and *gampi* on the right.

Using papyrus, the Egyptians created "paper" sheets by stripping layers and overlapping them at right angles and pounding them into sheets. The first written records were kept on papyrus in the form of pictographs. Courtesy: Kimberly-Clark Corporation

Kinds of materials used in papermaking: esparto on the left from North Africa, woodchips, and various kinds of cotton clippings.

An old engraving showing the various processes in papermaking.

Oriental handmade paper is made on similar flexible screens made of bamboo.

Western papermaking screens are rigid and made of fine wires.

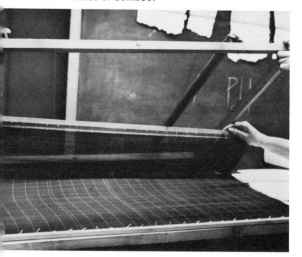

A small laboratory mill macerates cotton clippings into individual fibers in preparation for papermaking.

A vat of cotton fibers and water is being stirred to assure an even suspension of the fibers.

Jack Anderson of Andrews, Nelson, Whitehead has just lifted a mold from the vat and is shaking the fibers until enough water drains off to allow these cotton fibers to mat together.

He removes the frame from the mold . . .

. . . allows more water to drain away . . .

. . . turns the mold upside-down on a piece of wool felt . . .

. . . and covers the paper with another piece of felt.

He then continues stacking paper and felts. After this they will be placed in a press to dry.

Just as it was done nearly 700 years ago, a workman at the Miliani paper-making plant at Fabriano, Italy, shakes a screen by hand to drain off the water to form paper. Courtesy: Kimberly-Clark Corporation

A painting by Golda Lewis made of handmade paper and leather, 1963. Courtesy: Golda Lewis

trated the wax, After the wax was formed, graphite was dusted over the wax. Then an electrotype was made 1/32″ thick and was backed with ¼″ of lead. Fine wire screening was then pressed into the electrotyped object with burnishing tools. The wire took the shape of the electrotype and the result was a light and shade watermark. The old paper-making firm of Fabriano in Italy has mastered this technique. No difference of thickness can be felt when writing on these watermarked papers.

Laid Lines and Watermarks

In addition to the deckle, "laid lines" were also typical in handmade paper, because the pattern of the mold's screening subtly showed up almost as a watermark, causing a slight variation of a light and dark ladderlike pattern. There were from 24 to 32 fine brass wires to the inch.

Watermarks became marks of identification of molds and papermakers. Today they are usually trademarks. Watermarks are not marks made by water but were, at first, made with thread-thin wires stitched back and forth to hold a thin wire outline in place on the mold screen. Banknotes were made on watermarked paper to prevent forgery—until forgers mastered the process. The paper is slightly thinner where the watermark wires are, thus showing up when the paper is held against a light, much as laid lines are seen.

Watermarking developed into a fine art with the advent of light and shade watermarks. Portraits were modeled in wax that was poured on glass so that thickness and thinness could be observed as light pene-

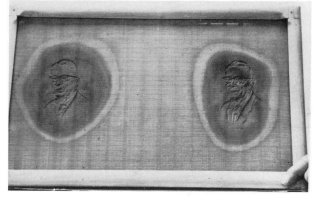

A screen showing an electroplated portrait that will become a watermark.

This photo was taken with light behind it to reveal a normally hidden watermark. This paper was made in Fabriano, Italy.

A piece of handmade paper with an Andrews, Nelson, Whitehead watermark. The paper is unpressed, revealing a rough-textured surface.

Machine-made Paper

Papermaking by hand is still being done in England, Italy, Japan, China, and India, to name a few places. Papermaking by machine, however, is a universal process and has come a long way since the first machine was made by Nicholas-Louis Robert in the early 1800s. But the principles of papermaking have remained the same.

The process begins when wood from forests or lumbermill waste shavings and sawdust are placed on fast-moving conveyor belts and are fed into a giant revolving drum called a barker. Jets of steam or water strip away bark and clean the wood. Next, a chipper, which is a revolving disk of sharp knives, reduces the logs to wood chips as big as cornflakes. The chips then travel on conveyors to ten-story-high rocketlike digesters or "pulp cookers." Steam and chemicals help to break down the wood chips rapidly into a soggy mush of cellulose and other wood elements. Chemicals, lignin, and resins are removed; what remains is pulp. The pulp passes through many cleaners and screens as it travels to the bleaching process. When bleached, the pulp is ready to accept coloring, sizing, or resins called the "furnish." The furnish makes for the finish.

Pulp, consisting of 99 percent water and 1 percent fiber and furnish, then enters the Fourdrinier paper machine. Pumps spray a thin film of pulp fibers onto a fast-moving endless wire screen. As the fibers travel along the screen, water drains away and the fibers mat together. Still damp, the paper is passed over a maze of hot rollers which press and dry it. Then, after more rolling, the paper is cut into various sizes and is ready for packaging.

Types of Paper

There are two basic kinds of paper—paper and paperboard. These differ mainly in thickness. Within these two areas, there are other classifications such as:

Papers

newsprint: basically ground wood pulp and a small amount (10 percent) of chemical pulp high lignin content which eventually turns the paper yellow and brittle

printing papers: ground wood and chemical pulps; pulps are bleached; sheets are sized, supercalendered, clay-filled, or specially treated for books, magazines, catalogs

fine papers: largely cotton fiber and chemical pulp for writing paper, bond certificates, money

coarse papers: ground wood and chemical pulps unbleached and made into heavy-duty wrappings, bags and shipping sacks, asphalting paper

special industrial papers: combinations of pulps with various pulp contents according to the specific need for abrasive papers, insulation, gaskets, filter papers, absorbent papers

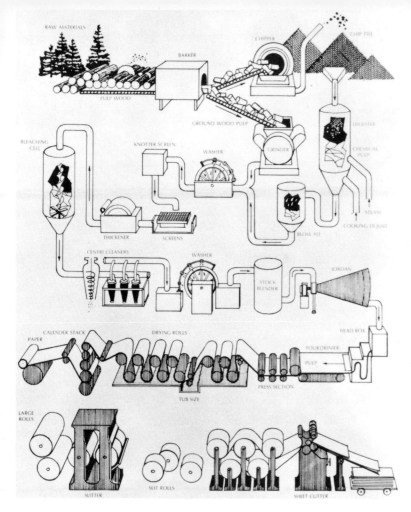

The making of paper today as it passes from one stage to another.
Courtesy: Boise Cascade

sanitary and other tissue papers: combinations of various pulp contents for paper towels, toilet tissues, facial tissues, wrapping tissues, pattern tissues

Paperboard

containerboard basically hardwood pulp but in some countries made of straw pulp—for corrugated material and fiber boxes

folding boxboard: combination of pulps and made on a cylinder machine where the outer surface of board is designed to take fine printing while the inner part gives bulk and rigidity —used for cartons for cereals, soap powders, etc.

special food board: made from bleached kraft wood pulp on the Fourdrinier and used to package moist and oily foods—milk cartons, frozen food packages, ice cream cartons, paper plates

set-up boxboard: made basically from wastepaper, thicker than folding boxboard—used for shoe boxes, candy boxes, jewelry boxes

other paperboard: combinations of pulps used for cardboard liners for gypsum board, tube and drum stock

wet machine board: so thick it has to be removed from the machine while still wet because it cannot pass through the dryers; used for shoe board and book boards

construction: combinations of pulps for roofing, floor coverings, automotive felts, and insulating boards

Within each of these categories are more fine differences of papers, some of which will be detailed in Chapter 2 and throughout the book when various processes are described.

A Paper Vocabulary

Paper was invented as a vehicle for writing. As a means of communication it has made invaluable contributions to history and civilization. But, unlike parchment and papyrus, paper can communicate without written words or symbols. A singe clean, flat sheet of paper offers promise that no words can begin to describe. Through folding, bending, rumpling, cutting, twisting, tearing, scoring, and curling, paper can be made to assume infinite configurations. Forms clean and subtle, and dynamic structures, permanent things, and paper fantasies meant for only a short life: all embody paper's purity. As a plastic material paper responds finely, the key to success being the correct choice of paper and tools.

Modern paper chemistry is making steady advances. Hundreds of papers have been developed to meet specific commercial and individualized needs. Paper is packaged in pads, rolls, sheets; different qualities and weights and raw materials help to define quite clearly the best purpose for each type.

Paper is described in several standardized ways. It is commonly sold in terms of weight. All weights are based on the weight of 500 sheets of paper, but different types are weighed in different sizes. Book sheet paper, for example, is based on $24'' \times 36''$ sheets, while writing paper is based on $17'' \times 22''$ sheets. Therefore, book paper described as 20-lb. paper would be very light compared to writing paper of the same weight.

Less common but equally valid methods of description include: *degree of strength*, the amount of resistance paper gives when we bend it, important in cutting or processing operations; *severance length*, the length at which, when paper is suspended from a high place, its own weight will cause it to rip; *degree of stretch endurance*, the point (measured in pounds) at which paper will tear when pulled from both ends; and *rupture degree*, the pounds per square inch required to rip it. But, more than anything else, exposure to different types of papers must be your guide.

It is important to consider what qualities a specific application will demand, since the quality of the finished product depends upon the paper with which it is made. Each type has different characteristics in finish, texture, color, thickness, stretching, erasing, and handling. Paper should be stored away from heat, excessive moisture, and direct sunlight, and finished products should not be subjected to excessive exposure either. Paper is extremely versatile, and it can be very durable if treated with respect.

Paper Grain

One very important consideration when working with paper is its grain. Paper made by machine is shaken side to side as it travels with the belt, and this has a tendency to align the fibers in one direction only. This is what is known as grain, and it determines why most paper tears more easily one way than the other. The fibers in handmade papers, however, are usually multidirectional, so these papers tear with equal resistance in all directions. Another factor is drying: handmade papers are allowed to dry naturally, while machine-made papers are dried on heated cylinders; this artificial drying yields a product that has not been allowed to shrink naturally. Grain is especially important where long or even strips of paper are required. When tearing strips of newspaper for papier-mâché, for instance, always tear along the length of the page. If you try to tear across the page, uneven, unpredictable pieces will result.

Several Aquabee art papers. From left to right: heavy-weight watercolor, Canvaskin, Super Vel, Venetia (100% rag), charcoal-pastel paper, heavy construction paper.

Two examples of double-sided papers. *Duplex* crepe paper by Dennison and *Reycote* two-sided paper. Both have different colors on either side.

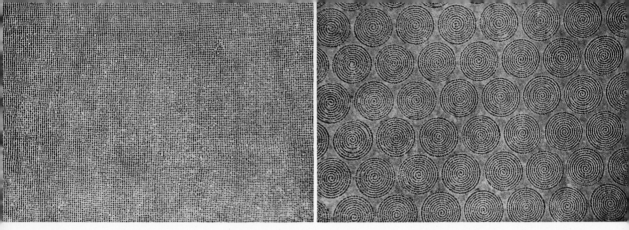

These four handmade Japanese papers are exceptionally light and fine.

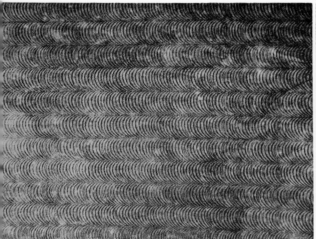
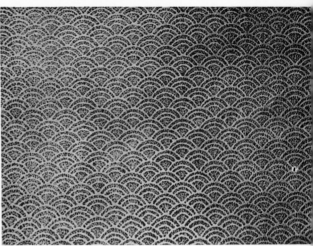

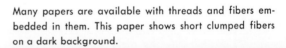

This fine paper was printed over with a light colored ink in a square pattern.

Many papers are available with threads and fibers embedded in them. This paper shows short clumped fibers on a dark background.

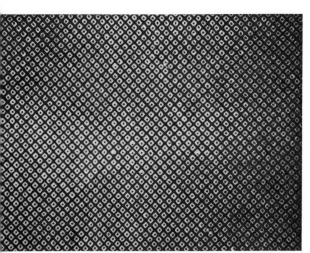

Although this paper looks as though it was printed, it is really a lamination of a fine light paper over a darker one—a testament to Japanese paper artistry.

When the strands become long and well distributed, as in this paper, they cease to be additions but become the paper.

The inclusion of small chunks of woods and grasses provides interesting texture in these papers.

Using the Proper Tools

The tools for working with paper are not elaborate. All of them are usually readily available, and most of them are so common that everyone has them.

For cutting, scissors, razor blades, and knives are very effective. If possible, have both large and small scissors on hand. Each has a specific function. Small scissors were not meant to cut large areas since it would take too long, and large scissors cannot be expected to produce the delicate cutouts used in fine decoupage. For long slits, a single-edged razor blade (or a double-edged blade with one edge taped) is fine, but an even more versatile tool is a razor knife, or a knife with replaceable blades. This type of

tool will aid in scoring as well as in cutting. Keep the cutting edges sharp by replacing them or sharpening them on a whetstone. You will find that cutting with razors or knives will be considerably easier if you have a workboard of soft wood, linoleum, cardboard, or many layers of newspaper.

Accurate measuring tools are just as important as sharp cutting edges. A good ruler is a necessity, and a compass, protractor, and triangle are often time-savers.

Other helpful devices are interim fasteners which are used to hold paper in place while the glue is setting or when you are cutting or folding another part. Clothespins, clips, and staples all serve admirably. And masking tape can be used this way very effectively.

Adhesives should be chosen with care; consider specific purposes and processes; for instance, is a rapid-drying glue necessary, will there be a great deal of tension, and will there be a need for very strong bond? Watery pastes and glues should never be used on large surfaces because they distort the shape of the paper as they dry. Rubber cement really makes the best all-purpose adhesive, and the excess can later be rubbed away from exposed surfaces. The basic white glues (such as Elmer's, Sobo, and Duratite) should be applied sparingly on small areas, except in decoupage and papier-mâché applications. They are very effective when used in the proper application, particularly where tension is present. One caution is against cellophane tapes as permanent or semipermanent adhesives. Most will yellow and crack, and unless the tape is well hidden or not a primary joint, it would be more professional to use another adhesive. If a tab is necessary as a connector, make one of paper and use an adhesive on both ends.

Using Tools Properly

Using your tools properly is as important as choosing the correct ones. Scissors, for instance, should always be held with the thumb through the smaller (upper) handle and the index finger below and in front of the lower hole; the middle finger goes into the lower hole. When cutting, keep the scissors as stationary as possible; with your free hand, manipulate the paper so that it is fed as continuously as possible into the middle of the scissors' moving blades. Of course, long straight lines may be cut with a knife, using a ruler to keep the edge straight. With thick boards or papers it may be necessary to make several passes with the knife; remember that it is not necessary to cut through a thick piece all at once. When scoring, be careful not to cut too deeply or the paper may crack when you bend it to shape. Also keep in mind which surfaces will appear in your finished piece; make any markings on those surfaces very light so that they can be erased later.

Paper Possibilities: A Vocabulary

The first chapter gave historical evidence of paper's use and its expressive possibilities. But only through experimentation can we really explore what potential these materials have for each of us. And only through systematic exploration is it possible to reach a deep understanding of any material's potential. Begin simply and directly.

BENDING

A single sheet of paper cannot stand by itself. It lies flat and empty. By simply bending a sheet and standing it upright, a three-dimensional form is created. This dynamic potential can be extended. Use a ruler to curve the paper gently in two directions. Space is further defined by the compound curve that the paper has accepted.

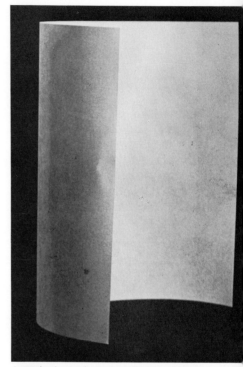

A single sheet of paper can become a three-dimensional structure by simply curving it and setting it on its long side.

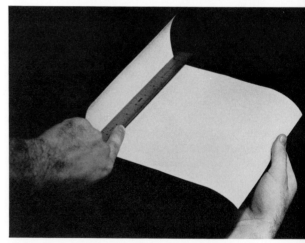

To give a piece of paper more permanent curves use a ruler. Pull the paper tautly under the edge of the ruler, or over the edge of a table.

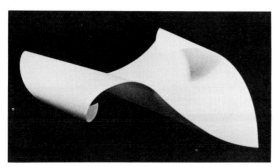

Do not hesitate to experiment. Curves can be combined in exciting ways.

WADDING

Wadding is another random alternative. Paper may be crumpled and creased to form crisp flat shapes. Aesthetic interest need not result from planned forms alone.

Wadding is another random technique.

CRUMPLING

Ignore for a moment the reasoned possibilities paper offers. Crumple a sheet. Crumple it again and again. Smooth it out, and crumple it once more. Note the changes that occur. After the first crumpling the lines are large and coarse; the paper is still thick and heavy. But the more the paper is kneaded the softer it becomes. The limit is a smooth sheet, because the more the paper is crumpled the finer its lines and creases will become. By continuing the process long enough a smooth, even surface will result.

FOLDING

By the same token, a form folded carefully has a better chance of providing dynamic interest when a specific effect is desired. Essential form rarely results from unplanned, unthinking actions.

Dynamic forms are hidden even in a single sheet of paper.

Crumple a sheet of paper. Crumple a stiff sheet, and crumple a thin, flexible sheet. Watch what happens as the sheets become more and more wrinkled. The paper becomes more supple and wrinkles are less pronounced the more the sheet has been crumpled. Think of this technique as a valid textural treatment.

BRAIDING AND WEAVING

Strips of paper folded together and into each other create still another effect. Braiding can be flat, or the technique can be expanded to weaving. Woven strips can also be allowed to remain two-dimensional, but by drawing them together space can be defined.

Three strips were woven into this flat braid. Also braid with more strips, thinner strips, thicker strips, paper of different colors.

Paper may be woven other ways, too. The warp here was made by making four slits in a large sheet and inserting strips in an alternating weave.

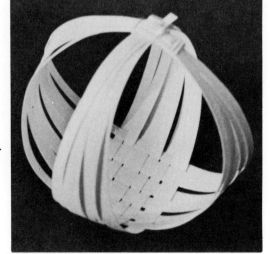

Weavings can offer three-dimensional effects as well. Strips woven and drawn together here define a sphere.

PLEATING

Pleating paper greatly increases its dimensional strength. Paper may be pleated along one edge, or diagonally. Many three-dimensional design possibilities are feasible with this technique. Lamps, furniture, and even buildings utilize this structural principle.

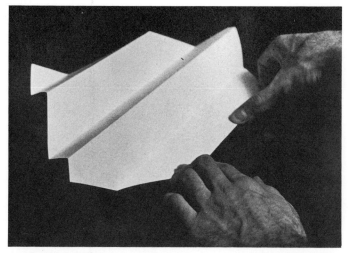

Pleat paper by folding it in opposite directions at even intervals.

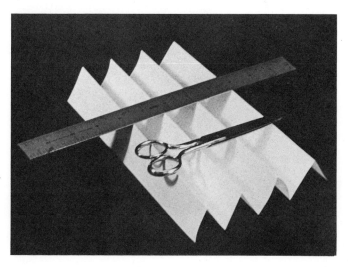

Pleating greatly increases paper's strength.

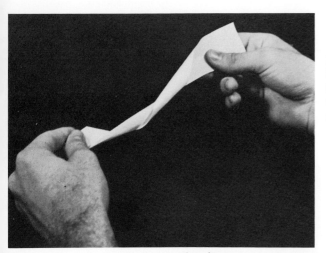

Papers may be twisted to shape.

TWISTING

Pulled and twisted paper offers other opportunities to define curved spaces. If a strip is twisted and pulled it will often assume a shape by creasing. By twisting and gluing the ends together a smoothly flowing form may be created.

This form was created by twisting a piece and joining the ends. A Mobius strip, this form has only one side.

PUNCTURING

Rough puncture holes and slits provide dramatic results. The jagged, raised punctures contrast very effectively with the smooth white surface of the paper.

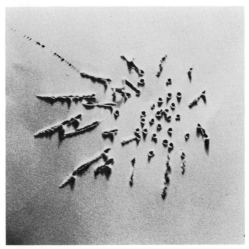

This ripped and punctured surface is expressive, a strong surface.

TEARING

Forms torn from a single sheet show counterchange possibilities. Rhythmic repetition of torn pieces can also be achieved by folding a piece once, twice, or several times and then tearing. Sections torn from a sheet may be set in relief, too.

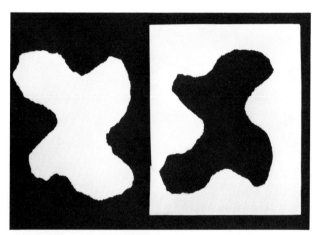

Torn papers show counterchange possibilities.

Torn elements may be curled. Once more, counterchange is an important element.

Decorative designs can be torn from a single sheet that has been folded once, twice, or many times.

CUTTING

Cutting offers a great range of effects. Shapes may be made from cut paper, and shapes may be cut out of paper sheets. The paper itself is transformed by cutting, as when a fringe is made.

Shapes were cut from paper using a razor knife to create this design.

Always cut by feeding the paper into the moving blades of the scissors.

Cutting can completely transform a sheet of paper. A flapping fringe bears little relation to the sheet it was cut from. And it is through many such transformations that important results are achieved.

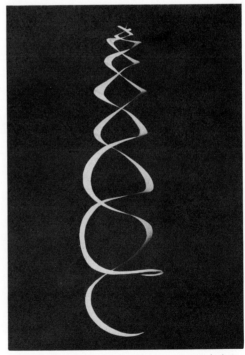

A paper circle was cut so that the paper spiraled in two strips from the center.

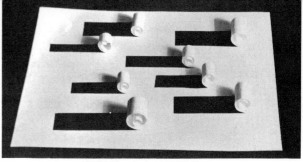

CURLING

Strips of paper may be curled by drawing the paper tautly over the dull outside edge of a scissors or knife. The use of several techniques yields further potentials. Paper can be curled up or down, as part of a larger piece, or as a piece in and of itself. Curls may be tight or loose, regular or wavy.

Strips of different lengths were cut and curled.

Curl paper strips by drawing them tautly over the back side of a scissors. Curls can be concentric or spiraling, tight, loose, even two-directional.

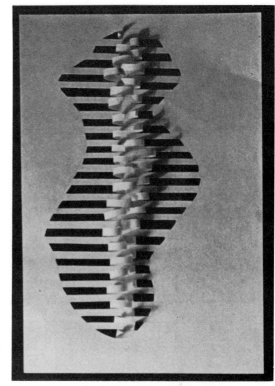

Curls meet at the spine of this design.

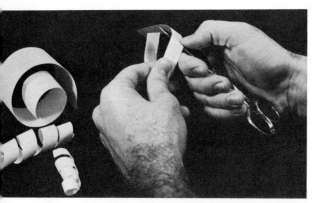

Sections of this sheet were curled and passed through themselves by making two slits in each one.

Gently curled tentacles reach out from the paper.

SCORING

Some papers, like Scorasculpture (Dennison), are meant to be scored. Score with almost any pointed tool. Knives and scissors work best. Always be careful not to score too deeply; the purpose of scoring is to open one side of the paper so that it will bend cleanly along that line in the other direction, with the scored line on the outside. Parallel or consecutive lines on a single sheet are often scored on alternate sides of the paper so that finished pieces have peaks and valleys. It is possible to create curves from a straight flat piece of paper.

Curved forms may be scored on alternate sides as well.

Score by drawing a knife or pointed object along the paper, and then bend gently along that line. Be careful not to cut too deeply.

These forms were made from squares scored alternately on either side of the paper.

Scorings and lines may intersect in different directions.

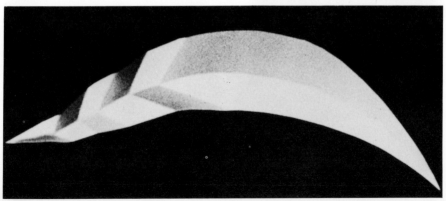

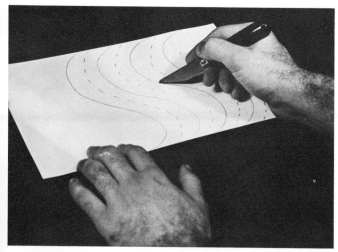

Larger pieces should be planned more carefully. Lightly sketch score lines first. Dotted lines indicate where the paper will be scored on the other side.

Scored surfaces can have high drama.

Bend the paper along the scored lines with the scored line becoming the outside of the fold.

A transformation is shown clearly in the case of the circle. A circle, with a slit to the center, forms a cone when drawn together.

Two scored lines transform the flat circle into the cross-section of three intersecting cones.

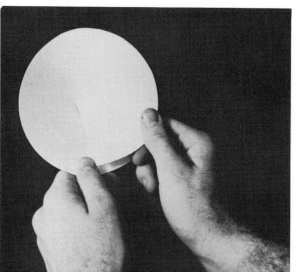

More scorings make the form more complex.

This form was created by cutting and scoring in two directions.

Cutting into the center portion further develops the same idea.

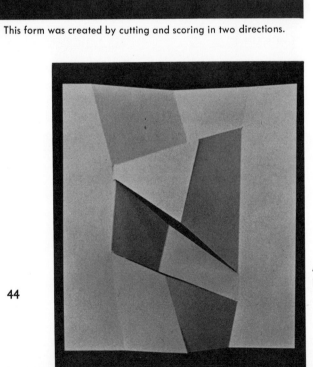

Another variation is to make each shape irregular.

44

A single slit and four scored lines produced this architectural relief.

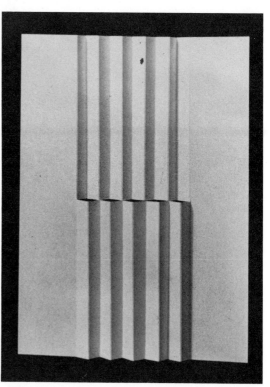

The same slit and more scoring gave rise to another development.

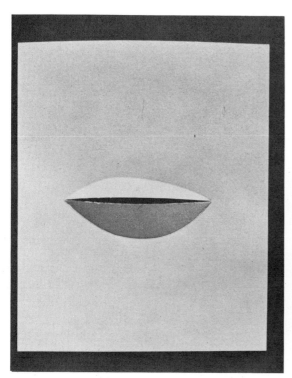

Curved scored lines bring relief shapes from the surface.

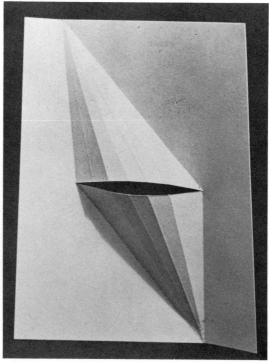

A series of straight lines here approximate a curved shape.

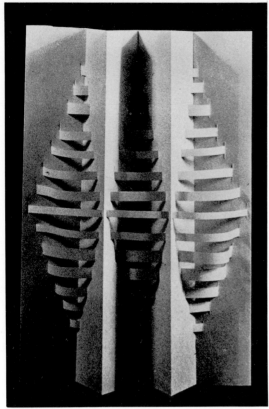

Paper scored for pleats was drawn together by thin strips of paper describing one possible combination.

Forms echo and repeat effectively.

SURFACE TREATMENTS

Combinations of these techniques are the essence of papercraft. The creative addition of forms and ideas is really the key point of these exercises. The few surface treatments shown here are important and valuable only insofar as they provide points for departure for your own explorations with paper materials.

Random windows open on both sides of the paper.

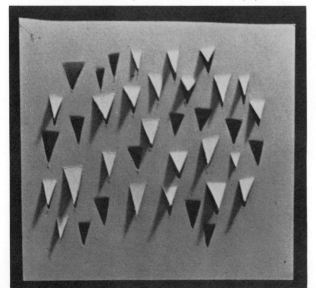

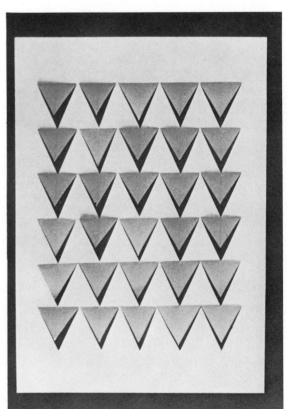

Another variation utilizes the same basic unit at regular intervals.

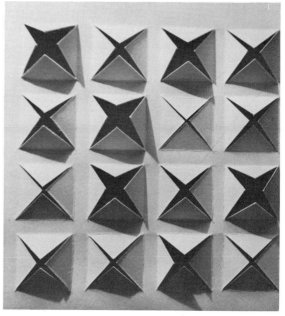

This form is transformed by varying the amount of open space in each square. Here the sections are nearly closed.

Further interest is generated by opening the spaces.

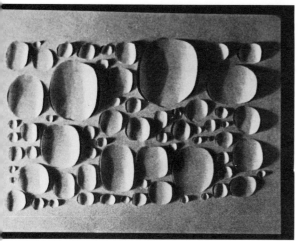

Circular forms were cut (leaving bridges at either end) and curled to raise them from the surface.

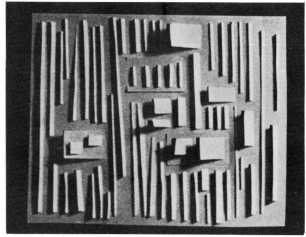

A low relief of long thin openings in the shape of an extended u is folded back like a shutter.

The stand on the left was scored and bent along two ends. The one on the right was slit and the flaps turned out in opposite directions.

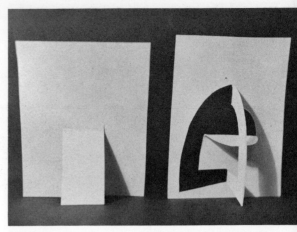

The three-legged frame on the left is supported by the middle piece. The frame on the right is the stronger structurally.

STANDS

Many stands for frames or photos can be made with paper. Some are more permanent than others, and with a basic idea of how to construct them—and an eye to your purpose —they are easily made.

FASTENERS

Papers may be fastened mechanically with and without adhesives. One way is to use metal fasteners, but strips can also be bound in a flat tie, or they may be fastened in a number of other ways by using tabs and slits.

Four basic ways of attaching paper strips.

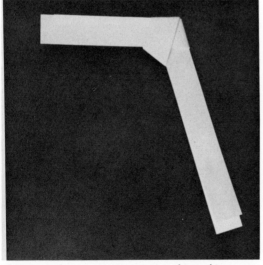

This paper knot is a unique way of attaching paper strips.

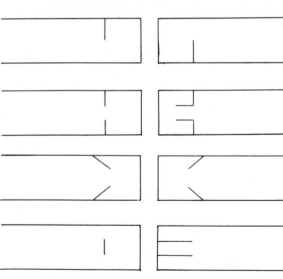

A. The slits are fitted together in this simple joint. B. Two tabs fit into the slits of the left-hand strip. This joint will accept more tension. C. Once more, the slits together. D. The center tab of the right-hand strip slides into the slit on the left. This joint is best reinforced with glue. It is useful when a strong joint in a continuous strip is necessary.

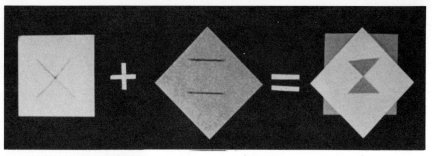

A series of joints like this could be used to hold large pieces of paper together without adhesives.

Two more surface joints for square pieces of paper.

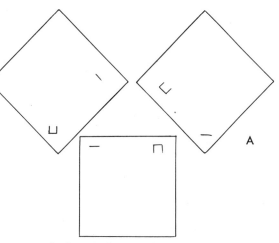

A

A. Fit tab through slit in each square. B. Fit the slitted squares together in the order shown.

B

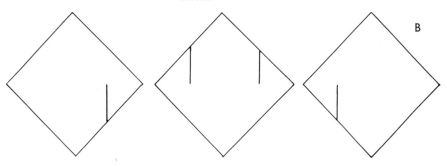

KINDS OF PAPERS

ART PAPERS	WEIGHT	CHARACTER-ISTICS	TEXTURE AND COLOR	USES
Arches	various weights	100% rag	wove finish, white or buff	printmaking
charcoal and pastel papers	medium	100% cotton fiber, holds charcoal and pastel dust	various colors, a rough-textured or line-textured surface	charcoals and pastels
English etching	medium	100% rag	antique surface, white	etchings
German etching	heavy	100% rag	wove finish, white	etchings
Hoshoshi	medium	made of *kozo* mulberry, largely free of wrinkles	white, fine-grained, soft	once was the ceremonial wrapping paper for the samurai and a ceremonial writing paper; used for wood and block printing
Ingres	medium	fine imported paper	full range of colors	charcoal, pastel, crayon
Japanese etching	medium	handmade	one side smooth, tooth on reverse side, off-white	etchings
Kochi	medium	opaque	soft, white	printmaking
Moriki	medium	handmade, laid paper, strong	soft, white	printmaking
mulberry	light	made of mulberry bark	slightly fuzzy surface, white	printmaking, decorative papers, rubbings
Natsume	medium	native swirling green fibers throughout	off-white, blotter texture	printmaking, decorative papers
Rives	various weights	100% rag	antique finish, white or buff	fine for all printmaking purposes
Scorasculpture (Dennison)	medium	easily scored, must be scored to be folded, very workable	very white, smooth, also black, silver foil, and gold foil	paper sculpture, forms in relief
Torinokogami	various weights	a combination of *gampi* and *mitsumata*, strong, long-life	yellowish, smooth, glossy	cards, colored paper, art printing paper
Unryu	medium	tissue containing fibers visible on both sides	white	printmaking, decorative papers
watercolor paper	a full range of weights	100% rag, can be stretched over a frame, withstands wetting and sponging	very white, rough	watercolor painting

KINDS OF PAPERS

GENERAL PAPERS	WEIGHT	CHARACTER-ISTICS	TEXTURE AND COLOR	USES
bogus drawing paper	light	uncoated, best for pastels, pencil, and crayon	middle gray value, rough	used in fashion design sketches
construction paper	medium	low-priced, easy to work with	full range of colors	multipurpose
Danshi	heavy	made of *kozo* mulberry, hand-made, tough, long-lasting	white, heavy long thick fibers used	ceremonial, ornamental wrappings, decorative papers
Fabriano cover	light or heavy	imported, deckle on four edges	available in 30 colors	paint, ink, pencil, decorative
flint paper	light	coated glazed paper	glossy, available in 70 colors	package designs, displays, cutouts, posters
Gampishi	light	strong, insect-resistant	yellowish, glossy	writing, origami, drafting, book covers, also tracing paper
Kamiko	medium	*kozo* mulberry is processed so that the fibers intersect to form crosses	white or stained with persimmon juice or embossed, crushed by hand to make it soft	once used as paper underwear and short coats, decorative uses
kraft	medium	strong	brown	wrapping, packaging, sketching, general purpose
manila drawing paper	medium	inexpensive, good for all dry media and ink sketches, but impermanent	buff-colored, heavy-toothed	pencil, chalk, pastels, crayons, brush, ink
Minogami (Shoin)	heavy	made of *kozo* mulberry, translucent, hard, compact, permits air flow	white	used as stationery and in *shoji* screens
newsprint	light	low-priced, best for dry media, usable with inks and watercolors	slight tooth, light gray	drawing, outdoor sketching
oaktag	heavy	strong, folds without cracking	a full range of colors	posters, booklet covers, paper sculpture
parchment	light and heavy	translucent	off-white, smooth	scrolls and diplomas
ruffmeal drawing paper	medium	similar to manila but with texture of fibers	cream, oatmeal finish (rough)	pastels, chalk, charcoal, watercolor
vellum	heavy	rag content, extremely transparent and strong	transparent, smooth	pencil, ink, crayon, watercolor, originals or tracings

KINDS OF PAPERS

SPECIALTY PAPERS	WEIGHT	CHARACTER- ISTICS	TEXTURE AND COLOR	USES
Albanene	light	100% rag, trans- parent, easily erasable, will not yellow or crack	white, smooth	tracing
carbon transfer paper	very light	carbon on one side	available in many colors	transfers
crepe paper	light	rolls or sheets, readily workable	crepe texture, a full range of colors	paper flowers, decorations
Duplex Crepe paper (Dennison)	light	comes in sheets, crepe with a different color on each side, very good body, very workable	crep texture, a full range of colors	decorations, paper flowers
graphite paper	light	coated with graphite on one side	graphite gray	tranfers to board and paper
gummed paper	light	gummed on the back	a full range of colors, smooth, matte, or glossy	paper mosaics, paper cutouts, general paper- crafts
metal foil paper	light	paper backed with metal foil, holds creases well	a full range of metallic colors in matte and glossy	decorative, paper sculpture, orna- ments, containers
stencil paper	medium	very tough	oiled or waxed	for making stencils
stick paper	light	pressure-sensi- tive, adhesive on back	opaque white, matte or glossy	address labels, masking
tissue paper	very light	transparent, very thin	full range of beautiful colors	collage, paper flowers, decora- tions, covering for papier-mâché and kites
two-tone paper	light	a different color on each side, Reycote and Dubl-Hue	a full range of beautiful colors, smooth, matte	decorations, gen- eral paperwork
velour paper	medium	a flocked paper	a full range of colors, a velvet surface	decorative trim, pastel painting

PAPERBOARDS	WEIGHT	CHARACTER-ISTICS	TEXTURE AND COLOR	USES
aluminum-centered board	light	dimensionally stable, usable on both sides, good for precise work, easily scored and shaped	smooth, white	pattern making, architectural renderings, technical illustration
bristol board	light to heavy	high or 100% rag content, tough, long-lasting, available in many thicknesses designated by the number of "ply"	very smooth, white	sculpture, pen-and-ink, posters, wash drawing
chipboard (newsboard, tarboard, Davey board)	light to heavy	dense, hard, uncoated	medium rough, gray to black	in bookbinding used for covers, .118" a popular size
corrugated board	light	corrugated, light	smooth or corrugated, many bright colors, some with patterns	wrapping, packaging, displays
Darby board	heavy	dense, hard	rough, white	posters, illustrations, tempera, watercolors, pencil
featherweight board	light	plastic foam cored, good strength, lightweight	smooth, kraft or white	models, displays, posters
illustration board	light to heavy	rag content, lies flat, consistent working surface	white, grays, black, different textures	illustration, commercial art
polyester-centered board	light	dimensionally stable, usable on both sides, good for precise work, can be rolled for handling	smooth, white	architectural renderings, pattern making, technical illustration
poster board	medium to heavy	clay-coated colored paper on laminated backing board	satin, a full range of colors	signs, takes airbrush, silkscreen, pen-and-ink, and many printing processes
railroad board	heavy	colored on both sides, very hard	smooth, a full range of bright colors	posters, mountings, displays

KINDS OF ADHESIVES

ADHESIVE	CHARACTERISTICS	USES
Duco cement	flexible, waterproof	all-purpose
epoxy	clear, exceptionally strong, usually comes in two parts, must be mixed and used immediately	used for making paper permanent
glue sticks	available in stick form, very tacky, often very strong	fine for adhering tabs and small areas
LePage's Original Glue	natural base, very strong, resistant to changes in climatic conditions	general paperwork
library paste	a strong but nonpermanent paste	good for temporary paperwork
Metylan cellulose paste	an inexpensive cellulose paste, dissolves in water	papier-mâché, collage
mucilage	amber color, tacky and syrupy	cardboard, woodwork
plastic glaze (Mod Podge, Art Podge)	white, dries clear, strong	good for protecting paper surfaces, acts as a finish over papier-mâché, etc.
polyvinyl acetate (Elmer's, Sobo, Duratite, etc.)	white, dries clear, strong	good adhesives for small areas, especially under tension, used in decoupage and papier-mâché
rubber cement	transparent, dries quickly, excess easily rubbed away	excellent for temporary and permanent bonds, good for large areas

chapter 3

Paper
in Two
Dimensions

From delicate hand-cut silhouettes to bold torn-paper weavings, the concepts of two-dimensional design in paper utilize several of the most basic paper-working skills.

Drawing, folding, cutting, rubbing, printing, gluing, stretching, weaving—these are the basics with which to begin designing on flat surfaces. They can be applied to pure art forms and exploration of design and to very practical and useful objects, as seen in the final chapter.

Of course two-dimensional paper is the base for paint and ink. But only the particularly special graphic uses of paper—like printing with a paper plate (collography) and making rubbings—are described here.

Working in two dimensions not only pre-

pares the craftsman or artist for passing into the realm of three-dimensional construction, but permits him to deal with many of the essential components of design—the elements which make a design "good" or "successful," or even "well applied."

It is advisable when working in two-dimensional design that you think of the paper and applicable design concepts as you create. What is the motion of the cutout? Does it flow, or is it abrupt and choppy? Is the weaving smooth, meshing, and geometrical? Or are the woven lines coarse, disjunctive, and lacking structure? How do negative and positive shapes work together?

The textures of papers, the ways of cutting, the positioning of elements within a

This untitled paper "painting" of sliced billboard poster is by Pavlos. Courtesy: Fischbach Gallery, New York

In preparation for printing, a printing plate is made by cutting mat board into the desired shape, coating it with acrylic gesso and modeling the gesso. After the gesso dries thoroughly, you are ready to print. Lida Hilton soaks the printing paper, and then dries it between blotters until it is just moist. The etching ink is heated and the printing press is adjusted to accept the thickness of the plate. Ink is rolled out on a sheet so the brayer can spread it evenly.

pattern, the relationships between light and dark, the use of color—these are a few of the concepts and values which should be considered when working in two dimensions with paper.

Printing with a Paper Printing Plate

A contemporary method of printing is collography. The result is a print with a low relief. A collograph is made from a printing plate composed of an assortment of materials which could be acrylic, gesso, cardboard, string, wire, mesh, cloth, buttons—almost anything. The plate is inked and printed to produce a print with shallow relief. In this case, the printing plate is oaktag, matboard, or railroad board. This background is coated with acrylic gesso and the gesso is modeled with a palette knife.

From printing plate to print, the product is paper. Lida Hilton's prowess with the process is detailed here with step-by-step photographs.

The ink, which has been mixed with a bit of extender such as Crisco (for better flow), is applied to the plate.

A piece of mat board is used to move the ink into the crevices. Then a piece of tarlatan (soft cloth) is used to wipe off excess paint and distribute it evenly.

Newspaper is used to highlight areas by wiping away more ink. For a second color the process is repeated.

The first plate is placed on the press over a sheet of oaktag that had previously registered the exact location.

The printing paper is taken out from between the blotters. Lida Hilton then places the moist paper over the inked paper plate.

A blanket is placed over the whole and the press is rolled.

The plate is removed but the paper is still attached in place under part of the roller and a second inked paper plate is placed between register marks on the bed. Both paper and background are put in place and rolled through the press.

An impasto effect comes through because the paper is damp. If it were not wet, it would not pick up the image.

Another collograph made with the same process by Lida Hilton.

The result is in relief from paper plate to paper sheet. Lida Hilton's completed print is in two colors, red and black.

Two collographs by Lida Hilton.

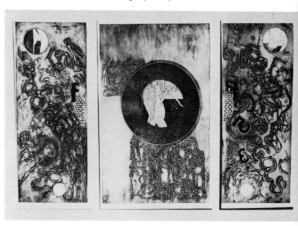

Paper Rubbings

Rubbings are a great way to bring the monumental sculpture home and to record great carvings. Most of us have made rubbings—by placing a coin under paper and rubbing the paper with a crayon. Rubbings provide a two-dimensional way to see pattern and texture.

All that is required is some printer's ink; a tamping pad of soft cotton wrapped around a wad of absorbent cotton with which to apply the ink; and a soft, strong, flexible paper that will accept water without tearing easily and will stretch somewhat in crevices and over bumps.

Some skill is necessary. Take care not to gum up the works with too much ink, or to tear the paper.

In the following process, a special Japanese sumi rubbing kit called *Bokataku* was used. It makes life easier but is not essential. Printer's ink and a homemade tamping pad will give the same excellent results.

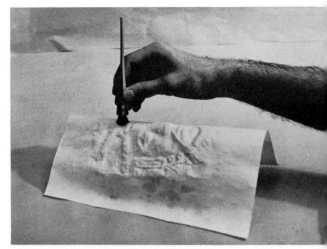

With fingers or a soft brush, tamp the paper into crevices at least partway to expose the part that is raised and to distinguish it from indentations.

Printing ink is being added to a composite in the *Bokataku* kit.

Dampened paper is placed over the sculpture that is to be translated into a rubbing. The paper should only be slightly damp—not wet, or else it will tear in the next step.

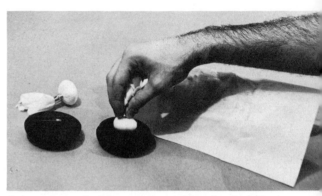

Make a tamper by filling a square of handkerchief-thin cotton with cotton batting and taping or tying the cotton cloth tightly around the batting. Dip the tamper into the ink supply, making certain that it is distributed and does not saturate just one spot. If this happens, take the ink off the first tamper with another one and use the second tamper instead.

Apply ink with an up-and-down motion until the entire configuration is revealed.

Remove the paper carefully and place it between sheets of newspaper to dry and straighten. After straightening, it can be pressed and rolled.

The finest details are revealed in this rubbing of a Mayan head.

A 20th century rubbing of a Chinese leather stencil of Tai Tsung horse. 76¾" × 50⅜". Courtesy: The Metropolitan Museum of Art

A rubbing from metal of two Thai dancers. Courtesy: Brimful House

Cutting from a Folded Circle

Folding and cutting creates a repeat design which has a very satisfying completeness. A circle of paper, while it can be cut in its flat form, is much more difficult to cut symmetrically than a circle which has been folded in half, in half again, and in half a third time.

This slice of the circular paper pie, when cut from both sides and unfolded into a circle again, shows the value of the fold.

The thickness of some papers may be prohibitive for cutting a folded circle. To overcome this problem, draw the design you plan to cut from the folded circle, take the tip of a compass or needle, and sink dotted lines through the entire thickness of paper. In this way, as you cut away several layers of the paper that are to be removed, a pierced dotted line will remain to guide you. It is a type of multi-thickness tracing technique.

The result, when unfolded, could be a doily, or, on a much grander scale, could even be a tablecloth.

Another Chinese rubbing of Lohan Ta Mo (Bodhi Dharma) seated under a tree. 31″ × 12″. This was probably made from a woodcut.

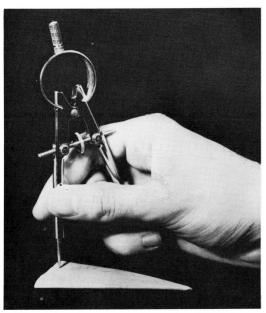

Cut into the layers of the folded circle with a sharp knife, following the dotted line.

After folding a paper circle in half, in half again, and in half a third time, draw a design on the folded paper. To "trace" it through to layers which cannot be cut through in one cutting, create a dotted line by piercing the folded thickness with the tip of a compass or a needle point.

Unfold and inspect the circular cutout. The symmetry of the form is appealing in a roundabout way.

Such folds and cutouts were employed to make this fabulous lacelike Mexican paper tablecloth.

Mon-kiri

A Japanese paper folding and cutting art called *Mon-kiri* has a long history founded in family crest making. The Japanese Samurai warriors, who took great pride in the decorations on their armor and banners, would adopt a design as a family crest. *Mon-kiri* was the art by which many of the Samurai crests could be made of paper.

Translating a basic geometry from nature (Japan's imperial crest is a 16-petal chrysanthemum which is popularly made from *Mon-kiri*), folded paper lends itself to just such repetition of internal design.

Squares of paper are folded in half diagonally, and then into two, three, four, five, or six folds. An outline is then drawn on the final fold and the form is cut out. If you experiment with drawing on the fold, you can create all kinds of designs.

To create the cherry blossom diagrammed below, start with a square of paper of a size which suits your purpose. Fold the square in half along the diagonal (Diagram 2). Starting from the midpoint of the diagonal, fold down a flap at a 36° angle (as the dotted line in Diagram 2 indicates and as Diagram 3 illustrates).

Fold that side again at a 60° angle (Diagram 4). Crease all the edges with the back of your fingernail to make certain that all folds lie flat. Finally, fold the opposite side back along the edge, hinging on the dotted line in step four. The result is the fivefold shape shown in Diagram 5.

Draw the design shown in Diagram 5 to make a cherry blossom. The striped portion is the design which is to be preserved. Unfold the cut paper, bringing the blossom into full bloom.

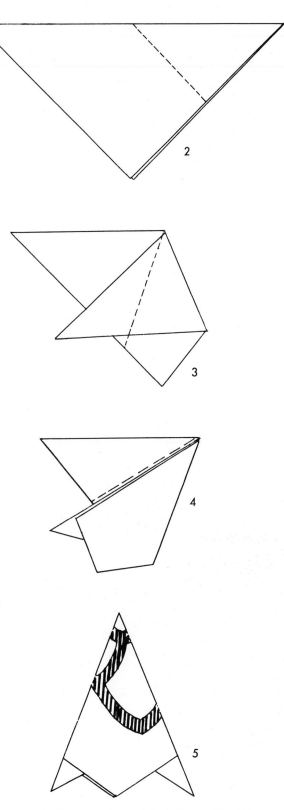

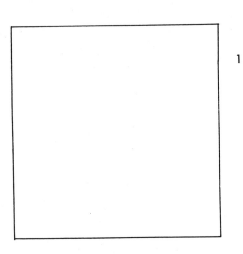

These are the five steps involved in folding a *Mon-kiri* form. The striped portion of the fifth diagram is the part which is to be saved after cutting. It will open to reveal a stylized cherry blossom.

The *Mon-kiri* cherry blossom and pieces of mother-of-pearl were decoupaged on this box.

Silhouettes and Symmetrical Cutouts

Silhouettes and symmetrical cutouts— both part of the fine art of paper cutting— have been used for centuries as decorations, votive figures, highly fashionable "portraits," love tokens, congratulatory mementos.

In mid-18th-century Europe, for example, silhouettes of faces in profile were highly fashionable. A person would have his shadow cast on paper, filled in with black ink, cut out, and pasted on a light-colored background.

Even earlier, in the 17th century, Swiss cut-paper designs and ornaments were commonly used as greeting cards, for holidays, births, expressions of love, and the like. Even today there are some Swiss silhouette-makers (who generally fold their paper in half for symmetry, reduction of labor, and balance of design) who are perpetuating the art of paper cutting. Nature's flowers, trees, animals, and children are all outlined in the fine flourishes of cut black paper.

Of course, in the cultures of the Far East, where knowledge of paper came very early, the methods for cutting and using paper evolved long ago as an art for the highly skilled.

On this continent, specifically in Mexico, the cutting of paper into symmetrical designs which have body and no internal design (the working definition of silhouette) has been important in religious and occult observances.

Although many silhouettes are made from symmetrically folded paper, which is then mounted on a background, the singly folded primitive paper idols of the Otomi Indians of San Pablito, Puebla, Mexico, are not really silhouettes in the traditional sense. They are not usually mounted on backgrounds. These symmetrical forms, although not nearly as polished as the European or Far Eastern versions, have a special purpose in the lives of the Otomi Indians.

As early as 1569, the Franciscan friar Diego de Mendoza encountered cut paper dolls which had been taken to the crater lakes of Nevado de Toluca where the Indians offered them as sacrifices, upon the mountain, to the gods of water.

These same cutout figures have survived as a living part of the Indian culture. Originally they were made only of cut and torn bark paper which the Indians said was the clothing of their gods. Each cutout still has a specific significance in the occult.

Out of black and deep purple bark paper the form of *Moctecuhzoma* is cut. He symbolizes the "evil air," a devil to whom most maladies and misfortunes are attributed.

The very powerful two-headed bird of the mountain, *Pajaro del Monte*, can banish all evil—even the wicked black-paper *Moctecuhzoma*.

Other light-colored cut paper forms such as the sentry and the "beds" on which the cut forms rest during ceremonies are essential in the Otomi customs.

For the "seed baptism" festivities, the Otomi cut papers which depict men holding corn, sugarcane, seeds, peanuts, chickens, birds, lambs, and all the other elements of a healthy farming year for which they make offerings.

These very positive hopeful forms are made of light colored tissue papers. White paper is used to relieve illness or misfortune in the specific cut forms of perforated corners, honeycombs, flowers, and a turkey egg. (The egg is thought the best symbol to counteract evil.)

But beyond counteracting evil with good cutouts, the *Brujo* and *Bruja* (male and female witches of the village) can inflict pain and do evil with the paper votive forms. Evil-working sorcerers, called *Hechiceros*, use black paper to cut out the figure of their victim, and pierce this two-dimensional design with pins or thorns. If a woman gossips too much, a witch may cut out her stylized form and press chewing gum over the paper doll's mouth—ironically combining the traditional votive custom with a contemporary oral habit.

But whether the cut form is Mexican and votive or Swiss and celebratory, all the makers of these silhouettes and symmetrical cutouts share that common art and craft skill of paper cutting.

As the Mexican figures show, any paper—coarse or tissue-thin—can be used in one-sheet cutouts. If working in the traditional European silhouettes, however, it is better to use smooth, thin paper.

Begin with a simple single fold and work with uncomplicated designs. As you progress and your skill and ability increase you can attempt different motifs with greater ease than if you began with an elaborate design.

The single fold, besides cutting labor time in half, automatically leads to repetitions of a design. This is itself a key aspect of the Swiss silhouettes' beauty.

You may also find that a preliminary sketch of your design will help. It is not necessary, however, to fill in every detail of the pattern. You will often want to work directly with scissors.

As you can see from the examples of silhouettes and symmetrical cutouts in this chapter, the cutting must be done slowly and meticulously to produce a fine result. Another factor, which is not evident unless you can watch a master at work, is the handling of the scissors. The hand that holds the scissors should not move around when sniping. The hand holding the paper should do the moving while the cutting hand is opening and closing the scissors from the same position.

Whether your design concept calls for elaborate floral embellishments or Otomi-type limitations of detail, keep your motif consistent. Be patient. The spacing of details, creation of fancy or flowing margins, regulation of horizontals and verticals within a design, and the use of light and dark mass should all come under your control.

A German silhouette depicting the summer season was cut from black paper. Notice the uses of masses of black and white, including the distribution of black around all four sides.

The Chinese, who are among the world's most skilled paperworkers, make fabulously fine, spider-web-thin silhouettes and cutouts.

Four-headed bird of the mountain, cut from bark paper by the Otomi Indians of Mexico, has the power to do good, according to the Otomi occult belief.

A singing Mexican rider bellows a flowery-sweet song in this folk art silhouette. Here the light paper is placed on a black background.

This Mexican silhouette was made by folding along a line between the two birds, and then cutting the design.

A single-fold cut paper doll which is wearing shoes represents the spirit of evil people. He does look rather two-faced at that.

The Otomi Indians offer up votive cutouts to the spirits of animals and seeds, hoping for good crops and cattle. This was cut from folded handmade bark paper, 9″ × 7″.

This silhouette of a stag and two hounds, cut in black paper mounted on white, was done by Hunt Diederich, a 20th century American artist. Courtesy: The Metropolitan Museum of Art

Folk Art Cutouts of Gummed Paper

In the nineteenth century, when the use of paper first spread to the rural areas of Poland, a fresh, amazing indigenous art form quickly evolved. Using sheep shears—hardly an artist's tool but nonetheless a replacement for delicate decoupage or silhouette scissors—Polish country folk began folding paper, cutting it, opening the folds, and pasting colorful papers on the cut repeat design.

This technique, now recognized as one of Poland's most fascinating folk art forms, has always been created by the farmland people for home decoration. Folded, cut, colored birds have adorned hamlets, barns, stables for years. Of course, as the quality of the paper art was recognized, the craftsman found that there was a commercial market for his expertise with the shears, besides wool. And, unlike many primitive artists, despite outside encouragement, these cutters have retained much of the freshness of design, adding only more color to the folk art cutouts. Unfortunately, because of the growing market found for the cutouts, the shearers no longer create for their own homes, but for the consumers.

The Polish paper cutters, despite the bulkiness of their tools, aim for and achieve precision of cut and contour. Like the Swiss silhouettes, the basic inspiration of Polish designs comes from either nature's flora and fauna or religious symbols. Fringed cocks, symmetrically flowing flowers, lace-winged angels all have a place in folk art. The cutouts sometimes represent joyous occasions like a wedding. But most of the time the cutouts emerge from different scenes in the farmers' lives.

Gummed paper works very well for making your own folk art cutouts. And you need not go out and find a pair of sheep shears. In fact, to achieve the precision of the Polish cutouts, you may do well to invest in a pair of tiny cuticle or decoupage scissors.

The farmers have long recognized the importance of the single fold. In fact, most of the Polish cutouts are done from pieces of paper which have a single fold.

Before the introduction of many colored papers, the Polish farmers made this type of single-fold symmetrical cutout, silhouetted on white paper or plaster wall.

After cutting out the folded form, unfold it, and cut equally precise pieces of gaily colored paper as internal design patterns and details. Lick and stick the gummed, colored paper in place. The Polish multicolored creations generally start with the darkest color, such as black, as the original folded and cut form, adding lighter color upon lighter color. Color is usually symbolic rather than naturalistic. This approach to color imparts a charm.

Besides Polish-type cutouts, gummed papers can be readily applied to other two-dimensional paper designs. *Mon-kiri* cutouts made of gummed paper are one possibility and pictures of various shapes can be made. Squares and rectangles of gummed paper can be arranged and overlapped to create a handsome contemporary mosaic-type composition. When working with cut paper designs, it is best to think in terms of planes of color or layers of planes of color as is apparent in these examples.

These twin birds were cut out at the same time using the single-fold concept. The bottom margin was folded in half before cutting, too. Notice that the colors were used in a steplike fashion, adding to the symmetrical look of this gummed paper art.

Finding most of their inspiration in nature, the Polish farmers make use of symmetry and bright color overlays in their cutouts. Courtesy: Cepelia

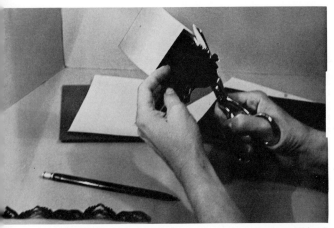

To make your own folk art cutouts, use a gummed-back paper. Draw a design on the folded paper, then cut it out. The Polish farmers use sheep shears and yet obtain remarkably precise cuts.

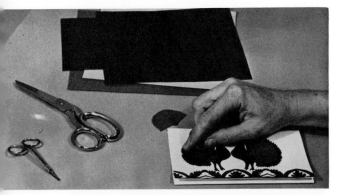

Lick and stick the cut gummed paper on a white background. In gummed paper of another color, cut pieces to be glued over the first cut layer.

This cutout, from the Lowicz region of Poland, shows how elaborate the talented craftsman can get even with bulky shears. Each of the Polish regions has its own style.

Gummed paper art can take directions other than folk art. Here it was used as the medium for an abstract composition.

In designing a mosaic, try to follow contours of forms and arrange the pieces in a dominant direction. Also vary mosaic shapes to correspond with the quality of what you are doing. Another possibility is to vary colors within colors—green can be represented by a range of greens, yellows, and blues much like the great mosaics of the past.

A paper mosaic, which can incorporate many different papers, including gummed, is another two-dimensional paper possibility. Cut pieces of colored and textured paper, and as you paste them down in your design, leave small lines of space between pieces for a mosaic look. Here the Pritt Glue Stick was used to coat the paper pieces evenly. A scissors helps in paper placement.

Paper Mosaics

Gummed and even non-gummed paper can be combined on a dark background to form a texturally exciting mosaic picture.

In paper mosaics, you may want to use the scraps left from other paper work. Be careful not to use too many different textures of paper in the design or the mosaic will lose continuity. Properly handled textures and colors can really unite the mosaic composition.

Real mosaics have spaces around them filled with grout. Here, however, working strictly in two dimensions, there is no need for grout. To simulate the three-dimensional mosaic design concept, leave small spaces between each of the paper pieces. This web of fine lines helps to unify the composition.

The Pritt Glue Stick is an excellent paper adhesive which comes in a lipstick-type form. It works well for neatly pasting down all the nongummed papers in the mosaic. Rubber cement works, but white glue may be too messy.

A purple-blue bowl containing yellow and orange flowers surrounded by multigreen foliage became a paper mosaic. Like the classic ancient Byzantine glass mosaics, several shades of one color can be used together to add dimension to the mosaic.

Design Suggestions

When working with gummed paper, silhouettes, and paper mosaic, the design idea is of utmost importance.

There are some simple approaches to two-dimensional paper design which can help you create a plan for that paper lying before you.

Start with a rectangle or square sheet of paper. See how many ways you can transform it using only scissors. One way might be to slit the rectangle into new forms that relate to one another but retain an essentially rectangular form. A sense of movement in the rectangle is achieved by repeating small elements of the design.

You might also try using curved lines on each side of the rectangle. Or divide the shape with only horizontal and vertical cuts. Other possibilities might be to cut concentric curves around three circular areas, imitating the grain in wood around knots, cut into only one side of the paper, and so on.

Now start with a triangle. Cut new smaller triangles from it, maintaining the integrity of the original equilateral triangle. Try changing the perimeter. Regroup the pieces. Modify the arrangement of triangles from a large triangle into stretched out S shapes, and so on. Playing with shapes is probably the best way of learning how to use them.

Try starting with the simple silhouette of a real object such as a fish. Depict it, and give it personality and life by cutting and respacing, using all the paper. Then try simplifying and abstracting until the fish is reduced to its most essential elements. Blank or negative spaces have a function—they become delineating lines.

Another design approach worth experimenting with would be to start with half of a representational form such as a leaf. Cut from this half-leaf the shapes that represent the internal order of the form—the veins.

Now fold back alternating slices of the design and you have counterchange. The blank-negative spaces on one side of the main axis become positive shapes on the opposite side of the vertical stem. This is a form of abstraction. Try it with other shapes. And try to apply some of these concepts when designing in two dimensions.

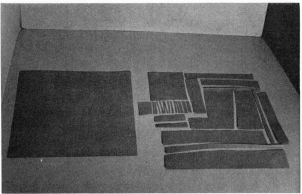

A square piece of paper can be cut and expanded into a design which has movement and interest.

Starting from the simple silhouette of a form such as a fish, add personality and identity to the cutout by cutting the fish apart. It is another simple but successful approach to design with paper.

An equilateral triangle takes on a new look when cut into an "explosion" of smaller triangles. This explosion technique is used on a decoupage box in Chapter 7.

The stylized shape of half a leaf can be turned into a negative-positive design. Cut the leaf along lines which approximate veins. Turn over every other strip to complete the full abstract leaf design.

Paper Molas

The Cuna Indians, a happy, handsome fishing people who live on the San Blas Islands off the eastern coast of Panama, are achieving world fame for their technique of cutting through layers of colored cloth, appliquéing and embroidering other colors in the cut-away spaces. This is called reverse appliqué.

The Cuna women, who are the artists, cut and sew layer upon layer of colored cloth, slowly revealing a story in design surrounded by multicolored strips of cloth.

Their molas are made of fabric and are worn by the women as blouses. These fabulous creations are adapted by others as pillows or they find places of honor on walls behind glass.

Genuine Cuna Indian molas are difficult to come by because they take so long to make. And, like the Polish paper cutters, the demand of an outside consumer market has an effect. For the Cunas, it has forced them to make less intricate designs at greater speed.

Their imagination is legendary. A photograph of parachutists jumping from an airplane inspires a mola of a clawed bee with a cockpit-head and opening parachutes all around. (The bee is striped with lines of color showing through holes from different layers of fabric). In another mola, two prizefighters—looking half stunned—box in the ring. All around the boxers are heads of animals, perhaps placed there as a Cuna woman's social commentary.

As a fabric art, the molas have an application for the Indians. But for us, the beauty of the cloth mola can be duplicated with colored paper as well.

Take a sheet of paper and draw a design on it, keeping some conception of parts to be cut away and colored with other papers.

With a sharp knife, cut away all the areas through which other colors should show. Now, working from the back of the mola outline, take pieces of colored paper and, spreading rubber cement around the outer edge of the hole to be covered, adhere the two papers.

After all the original holes have been covered with colored papers, cut away more spaces in the new colors and repeat the operation. Next add more intricate designs within these second colors by gluing new colors over these shapes as before.

The result is most effective and colorful. Like the Cuna cloth, it becomes a very expressive medium with paper.

To make a paper mola (a paper translation of the fabric technique of reverse appliqué), draw a design on a sheet of paper, and remove spaces with a sharp knife. To take inspiration from the molas of the Cuna Indians of San Blas, Panama, use primitive designs—like this airborne dragon. Also include dozens of horizontal lines which the Cuna women fill in with many different colors. The knife used here is a special one with a swivel so that it more readily follows and cuts curves.

Working from the back of the cutout paper design, cover parts of the mola with different color papers.

A winged dragon cruising among the stars has a colorful primitive charm.

Two-Dimensional Paper Weaving

Although not nearly so functional as cloth weaving, paper weaving done without a loom can be a real challenge to even professional weavers. Because of the multitude of textures, widths, colors, and patterns available in paper, weaving variations are limitless.

Weaving incorporates simple techniques which can be varied by changing the way the strips are interwoven, changing the way the vertical strips (warp) and the horizontal strips (weft) are cut and placed, using negative (open) spaces in the weaving, and so on.

Color and texture can enrich the surfaces to please the senses.

Probably one of the simplest weaves to perform is a regular alternating pattern of warp and weft strips.

Start by making the warp out of a sheet of paper. With a sharp knife and straight-edge, cut straight parallel lines in the paper, leaving an even margin all around.

The weft (horizontal strips) can be cut lengths of paper of another color. Weave the weft strips one at a time through the warp. As you add more and more of the weft, a checkerboard design will begin to appear. The completed weaving, if impregnated with polyester resin, could become a handsome place mat.

A variation on this simple weaving theme would be to take the same straight warp and weft design, but when weaving the weft through the warp, skip over some of the strands leaving longer bands of color. In the following rows, you can repeat or gradually alter this more irregular design, broadening the extra color areas, even weaving some specific figure outline into the form.

If you use longer strips of weft, the weft can be slightly raised into a relief pattern by looping in spots and then returning to the normal weave.

Try changing the warp. With a sharp knife, cut curving lines in the warp, retaining an outside margin. Weave straight weft strips through the warp to create an op art effect.

Try zigzagging the warp. And to add even more interest, cut slanted slits into the weft paper strips and weave other lengths of paper through these slits. Now weave the combined weft strips through the zigzag warp, as though they were one strip. It's crazy, but it gives some idea of the potential of paper weaving.

Vary the widths of the weft. Try different papers with different colors, textures, shapes. You can let the warp control your design, or you can give control to the weft, all depending on how you cut and interweave them.

Using unattached strips of paper, without the margins of the paper demarcating limits, set up a warp again. This time let either warp or weft dominate. Try making a warp of only a few strips laid side by side, spread out (to leave negative or open spaces), or angled askew from the parallel to give the weaving a sense of motion.

Now weave with the weft strips dominating. Sometimes alternate the weave, other times let the horizontal lines—or the vertical ones—show on top more often and for extended lengths. Leave some unwoven spaces. Don't necessarily make the ends of the warp and weft strips line up evenly—it can be part of the design to have the woven ends protrude randomly.

Try weaving with this same approach but using torn paper strips for both weft and warp. Let white space show through. Permit some color or colors to dominate. Tighten and loosen the weave. It's up to you. Paper weaving is as open-ended as you make it.

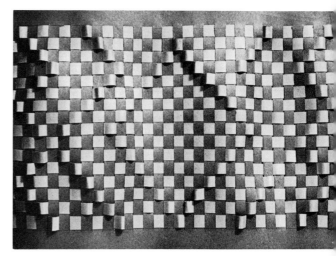

The weaving becomes a relief design by lifting parts of the weft.

To make a simple checkerboard weave, cut the warp (vertical strips) from a sheet of paper, leaving a margin all around.

Thread strips of equal width horizontally (the weft) in and out of the warp.

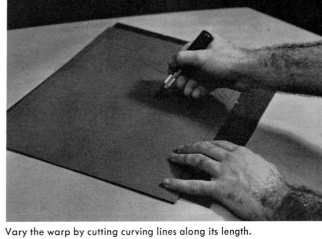

Vary the warp by cutting curving lines along its length.

This curvy warp can be woven with straight or curved weft. The straight weft shown here creates an op art design.

The weft in this weaving was made of strips which were slitted and woven with thinner strips. This weft was then woven into the zigzagging warp. Different width strips were also used in the weft.

Torn strips of yellow, red, and orange construction paper compose this irregular weaving. Tearing and controlling the density of weaving make this a texturally interesting design.

In a warp without a margin, designs can be more varied. Always set up the warp first; then add the weft. The irregular placement of the strips, the presence of some negative (open) spaces, the change of the angle of the warp, and the use of uneven margining of the weft are major variants of this design in glazed paper.

The warp is made of curved strips of white paper which are spread out and woven with alternating strips of gray and black. It results in a curious optical pattern. Simple weavings often look complex.

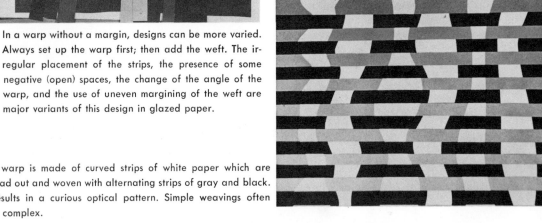

This woven paper headdress from Sierra La Puebla, Mexico, is part of a traditional dance costume. Pre-Columbian Aztecs and Mayans used similar woven headdresses. The warp is actually made of thin dowels with an alternating weft of various colors and kinds of paper.

chapter 4

Paper
in Relief

The moment a sheet of paper is cut, folded, curled, bowed, or otherwise brought from two dimensions into shallow relief, additional concepts of design necessarily come into play.

In two dimensions, the only way to achieve depth of design is through varying sizes of objects and using perspective. But in relief and three dimensions the sense of depth is real. By changing the depth of the structure, the artist uses light and spatial relationships to create essential forms.

Every form has a characteristic distribution of light across its surface. Angles have a sudden light-dark contrast; spheres will register in the eye and brain as a gradation from light to dark. Such values of light and shadow are first introduced when one begins to work with relief constructions. Light—without which there would be no design—determines how depths, textures, and other spatial values will reach the retina.

The positioning of planes in relief— as in paper tole or origami—is one key consideration in achieving spatial balance. As with two dimensions, look for variety, harmony, and unity in design. When working in relief and in three dimensions, consider the way light affects planes, curves, protrusions, spirals, and different degrees of depth. With paper or any other material, the third dimension is an exciting realm to explore.

When creating a scene, elements that are farthest away are placed higher up on the background. Similarly, those forms closest to you are positioned lower down. Of course, closer objects are always bigger.

When several prints are used, a degree of overlapping also enhances the illusion of three dimensions. Consider using several related prints and combining them into a new arrangement.

Usually, the entire piece is sprayed with a mat sealer and the piece is framed and covered with clean glass.

Mary Delany made a series of these flowers c. 1774 from cut watercolored paper. The designs are precise and made entirely of bits of colored papers.

A cut paper valentine from the early 1800s. Courtesy: Williston Memorial Library, Mount Holyoke College

This valentine in green and orange is a paper weaving dating to the early 1800s also. On the back is this statement:

> Many hearts ensnared
> All by a fickle *snarer*.

That was in the days when Valentine cards were sent by anonymous senders. Courtesy: Williston Memorial Library, Mount Holyoke College

Decorative Ornaments in Relief

A favorite design is the star or sunburst effect. It is a theme that has endured for centuries. Here are two more interpretations, one employing paper folding and cutting, the other paper curling and scrolling. Both are simple and effective and, best of all, permit great latitude in interpretation.

A third approach develops another popular theme, that of a wreath. Here again, there are limitless variations. The basic concepts here are paper cutting and scoring. Although not paper tole, the effect can be the same, except for the fact that the entire piece—from design to creation—is a result of your own imagination.

Fold a rectangle into accordion pleats. In this case each pleat is about 1" wide. The width should be in proportion to the size of the paper. This sheet was 12" × 16". Then fold the accordion piece in half. Repeat these steps to form a second piece that will be used to complete the other half of the circle.

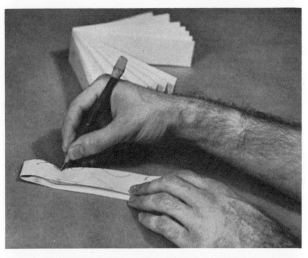

Draw the design you wish to cut out on both folded edges. Then cut away these shapes.

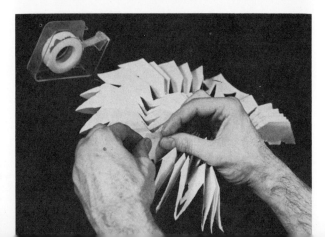

Open the two halves and attach the center with a paper clip or loose-leaf ring. Then join the edges with glue or tape to complete a circle as shown here.

The completed star-sunburst. Color, pattern, texture, and size are all variable in this technique.

Gold metallic paper embossed and scored was used to create this Portuguese ornament. Beads are used for flower centers.

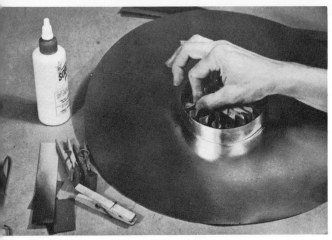

Gold metallic Scorasculpture was used to make this sunburst ornament. A base circle was cut first, then strips of two different widths were cut. Some were shaped into circles, others into loops, and still others into spirals.

White Scorasculpture was cut into a ring, flowers, stems, and leaves. The flowers were made by scoring concentric circles as described in Chapter 2, and the edges were cut into fringes. Leaves and stems were made by scoring.

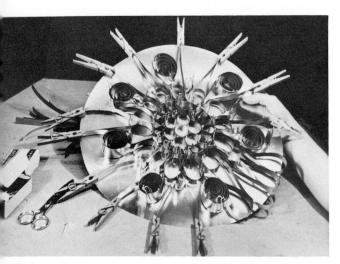

The pieces were glued and then clipped together with clothespins and paper clips to hold them in place while the glue dried.

The whole was assembled clockwise with Sobo to crea this relief.

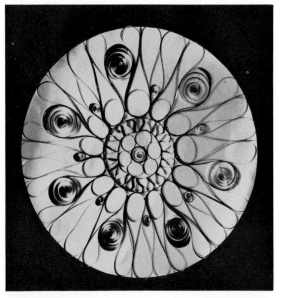

Almost linear from this angle, the ornament glows to create a decorative ambience in any room.

Folder Paper Container

Because paper is strong it is often used as protective wrapping. The Japanese have developed many ceremonial wrappings. The basic shapes are square and rectangular. The emphasis here is on simple folds with a minimum of overlaps.

The wrapping shown here is a flat one. It might be used for a card or papers or anything that can be folded relatively flat.

The finished form should resemble this.

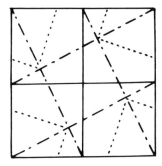

Fold the paper in opposite directions as indicated by the dotted and dot-dashed lines diagrammed here.

Use a thin paper that will crease easily, and fit the folded sections together as shown.

Three-Dimensional Realism or Paper Tole

Decoupage evolved as a paper cutting art into three-dimensional forms of Victorian paper pictures. Along the way were the innovations of people like Mary Delany (see section on decoupage) and others like her who filled their leisure moments by creating with scissors and paper. Out of this came temporary decorations for the house such as paper trims for windows and closets, for linings such as doilies, and for expressing sentiments such as Valentine Day cards.

As prints became more common, those who could not draw and paint re-created prints by dissecting them with scissors and reassembling parts in a new way to create three-dimensional effects. We have all seen childrens' books that open up to reveal a three-dimensional standing scene made of paper cutouts. The *vue d'optique*, paper tole, or three-dimensional arrangement (all terms for the same thing), works on that same principle, but with a more shallow depth of field.

Vue d'optique / paper tole / three-dimensional forms is a method of imparting relief usually using flat materials such as printed paper flowers, leaves, figures, buildings and assembling them in a shadow box of some kind, usually covered with glass. Duplicates of the same print are used. From a single print the foreground elements are cut out. Whatever remains becomes the background. And from one or two other prints, foreground and middle ground elements are cut away. If they are flowers, petals are sprayed with acrylic spray and when the parts dry each petal and leaf is molded or contoured in the palm of the hand. Use your fingers to stretch and form the paper into petal and leaf shapes. These are then assembled—background pieces first, middle ground next, then foreground and details. Some of these pieces need to be supported. The best and most modern material is RTV silicone seal adhesive. It is rubbery and adheres well. Assembled pieces can be built up with RTV silicone elevating the pieces as desired.

Three prints of Flemish flowers were used to create this paper tole picture by Maxine Ludden. Each petal is cut out, molded slightly, and adhered in relief. The background is silk moiré. Courtesy: June Meier of the Cricket Cage.

Gini Merrill designed this box combining old-fashioned prints with a Victorian scene.

Musicians by Jane Bearman. Hand-colored and cut papers over canvas.

Crepe paper flowers made with Duplex.

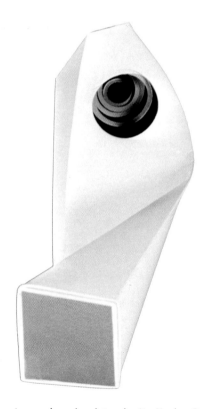

A paperboard sculpture by Jim Hanko. *Courtesy, Jim Hanko.*

An entirely handmade book covered with a hand-marbled paper.

A festival lantern from India.

Batik paper in a splash design.

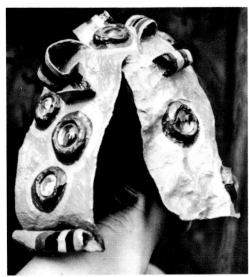

A papier-mâché headpiece with plastic cabochons incorporated in the design, by Ed Ghossn. *Courtesy, Ed Ghossn.*

Paper in reverse appliqué, inspired by the Cuna Indians' molas.

The classical piñata. *Courtesy, Fred Leighton's, New York.*

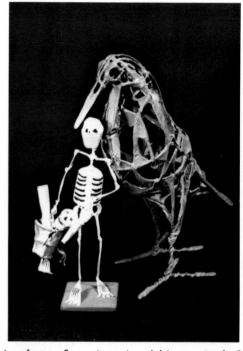

Mexican fantasy figures in papier-mâché over wire, by Saulo Moreno.

Polish paper cutouts. *Courtesy, Cepelia.*

A papier-mâché monster form blown up with firecrackers during Mexican religious festivals.

Lee Weber's three-dimensional fairylike garden made by surgically dissecting several prints and reassembling them in shallow relief. Courtesy: Lee Weber

Another variation on the same theme by Lee Weber.

Another interpretation of paper tole by Gini Merrill.

Patricia Nimocks created these shadow box tables using multiples of prints. RTV silicone sealer acts as a bulk support for the relief effect as well as an adhesive. Courtesy: Patricia Nimocks and Connoisseur Studios

Shadowbox table by Patricia Nimocks. Courtesy: Connoisseur Studios

Origami

Origami, the Japanese art of folding square pieces of paper into decorative or representational forms, can be simple enough for young children to do, although adults will find a challenge in making difficult forms. Hundreds of carefully folded possibilities—including swans, seals, cranes, peacocks, lobsters, boxes, hats, horses, penguins, goldfish—require careful attention to step-by-step folding procedures along with meticulous consideration of folding angles.

As with most paper art and craft, once one has tried Origami it becomes easier to give less thought to the individual fold and more to the entire creation. Here we include step-by-step illustrations for making a Samurai helmet, fish, flapping bird, and monkey. Although representing just a fraction of the Origami possibilities, these four forms do encompass most of the important folding processes. In particular, the "basic form," which must be made for both the flapping bird and the monkey, is the opening key to hundreds of other Origami creations.

Although there is specially made Origami paper on the market, almost any light paper which readily accepts and retains folds can be used in this folding paper art. All Origami products are made out of square pieces of paper. And it is important that the paper be exactly square, although the size of the square is of no import.

Dotted lines, in the diagrams which follow, indicate the lines of the folds for the next step. These dotted lines are an important clue as to the angle of folds.

SAMURAI HELMET AND GOLDFISH

A miniature Samurai helmet can be made out of a square piece of paper 6″ × 6″. (To make one which could actually be worn, use a piece of newspaper or other large piece of paper trimmed to a 20″ to 22″ square). Although they may seem a curious duo, a goldfish can be made out of the Samurai helmet with just three additional steps.

Fold the square in half along its diagonal as shown in Step 1. Follow the dotted lines in the first diagram, fold the two triangular ends of the folded square so that they meet, forming a smaller multifold square. This square has, on one face, two hinged triangles. These triangles should be folded back upon themselves as shown in Diagram 3.

Two flaps of these two folded back triangles are then folded out—deviating from the square shape which has been maintained to this point. Also in Step 4, you should crease the entire paper form along the two dotted lines. But do not permanently fold these creases yet.

Looking at the figure now from the back side of the hat (Diagram 5), perform the fold indicated in Diagram 6. This folding back of a triangular tip should be done on both sides of the hat.

Fold in the small flaps at the sides of the hat, and bend up the band shown in Diagram 7 to complete the Samurai helmet. You can omit the bending of the two small flaps shown in Illustration 7 if you want the sides of the hat to come to points.

To make a goldfish, follow the Samurai helmet directions. In Step 7, however, you should definitely *not* fold in those two small side flaps. Let them come to points—they will be trimmed into curves later.

After completing Step 8 (except for those points), fold the helmet in half along its line of symmetry, making the back of the hat (the side without horns) the inside of the fold. One horn should be on each side of the folded piece. But they are no longer horns—now they are fins.

Cut (do not fold) along the dotted lines in Diagram 9, as shown in the accompanying photograph. Having cut and rounded the goldfish, you will find that there are two relatively loose pieces of paper folded in the center of the fish's inside folds. Gently pull out these ends—they will become the tail.

If you pull them out all the way, these pieces will naturally lie under the fish as shown. All that remains is to trim the tail so that it has two lobes and looks "fishlike" by representational Origami standards.

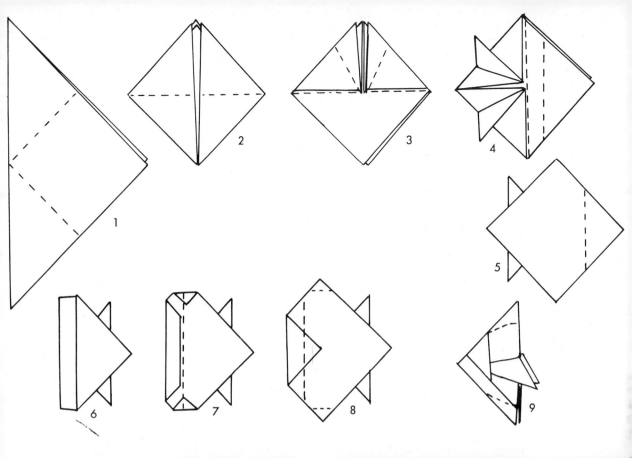

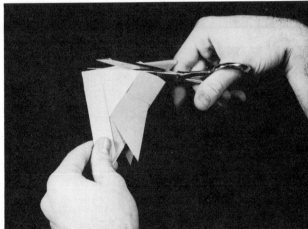

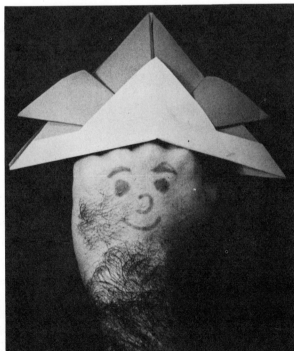

The heavily bearded and armed Samurai warrior dons his Origami helmet.

Trim the pointed ends of the folded-over Samurai helmet into curves for the fish.

From the inside of the fish, pull out the two loose folded paper strips which will become the floppy tail of a goldfish. Trim these tail flaps to form a two-lobed tail.

THE BASIC FORM

To make most Origami animals and birds, you must begin with a basic folded form. It looks like a stretched diamond, and has great versatility for making bodies, legs, heads, necks, and wings.

Fold a square piece of paper in half diagonally. Now fold it again into a smaller triangle as shown in Diagram 2. Crease along the dotted line which is shown in the second step, and then take one of the two hinged triangles and fold it into a square along that crease line (Diagram 3). Do this for the other triangle as well, creating a pair of joined squares.

In Step 4, fold the outside square on each side back upon itself. This will reveal a slit running down the middle of half of the form (as shown in Step 5).

In Steps 5 and 6, fold along the dotted lines on both sides of the half-split double square. This creates a lopsided diamond which still has the half-split. The flaps which are folded over should meet but not overlap along the slit.

Fold the entire thickness of the top part of the diamond so that it is well creased (along the dotted line in Diagram 7, shown bent over in Step 8).

After creating this crease, bring the form back to the lopsided diamond position of Diagrams 7 and 9.

The most difficult and important step in making the basic form is shown in Diagram 10. To "extend" the diamond shape to the final basic form, spread open the two flaps on one face of the form. Grasping the bottom tip of the form with the thumb and forefinger, and holding the tip of the topmost single thickness of paper with the other hand, gently pull out the form, releasing several folds, and creating an equilateral parallelogram (diamond) shape. Crease the two new edges of the diamond so that the form will lie flat along its center line. The paper ends should neatly butt, but not overlap.

Repeat this process for the other side of the form, creating a double diamond shape (Diagram 11).

Now that the basic form is completed, take a moment to study the result. One half of the double diamond is slit down its center. The other half, hinged along the shorter diagonal of the diamond, is easily bent down to reveal a protruding triangle. You will see how this half-slit/half-hinge form lends itself to birds and animals in the flapping bird and monkey creations which follow.

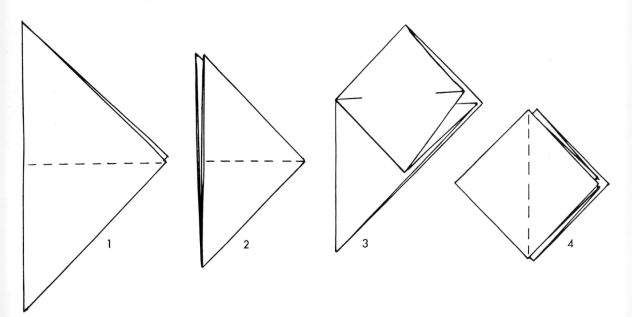

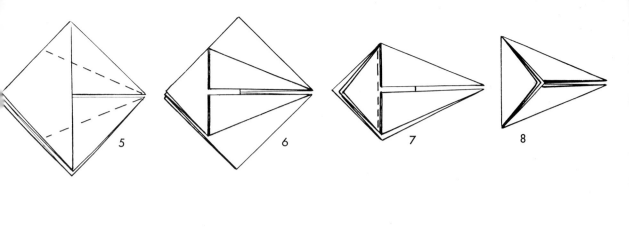

5

6

7

8

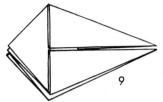

9

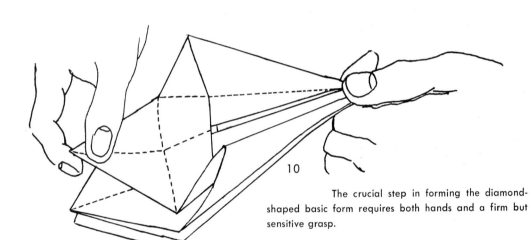

10

The crucial step in forming the diamond-shaped basic form requires both hands and a firm but sensitive grasp.

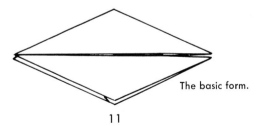

The basic form.

11

FLAPPING BIRD

Starting with a completed basic form, crease the form along the dotted lines shown in flapping bird Diagram 1. Make certain that these creases are made on the half of the basic form which is split. In this way the folded parts will be able to go in opposite directions when folded up.

After creasing, fold these strips so that they point upward and are set between the hinged flaps of the original diamond as shown in Diagram 2.

To complete the bird, perform the fold shown in Diagram 2 which becomes the beak of the bird. The tail end remains unaltered. Take the as yet untouched flaps of the original diamond and bend or curl them along the sides of the bird, to form wings.

This completes the simple flapping bird, but if you want to make him really flap, hold him by the base of the neck and base of the tail with thumbs and forefingers. Holding the neck still, gently jerk the tail end back and forth. This makes the wings really wave. Hang on tight for a bird's-eye lowdown on Origami.

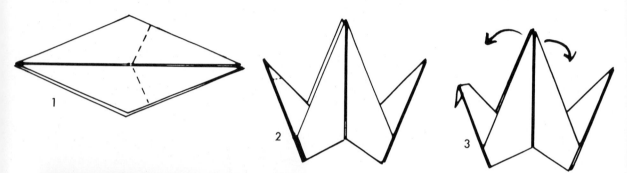

MONKEY

The monkey also relies on the basic form. This ape-tizing Origami creation requires two separate pieces of paper—one for the tail and legs, and another for the torso, arms, and head.

To make the upper half of the monkey, begin with the basic form folded on the split half of the diamond like the bird. The angle of the fold is slightly different from that used for the bird. This should be noted. In Step 2 fold along the creases so that both parts of the split half-diamond stick out perpendicular to the central line of the diamond.

Keeping up the symmetry, crease the two protrusions which will become arms as shown by dotted lines in Figure 3. In making the upper half of the monkey, ignore the dotted line in Diagram 3 which cuts across the top half of the original diamond—this

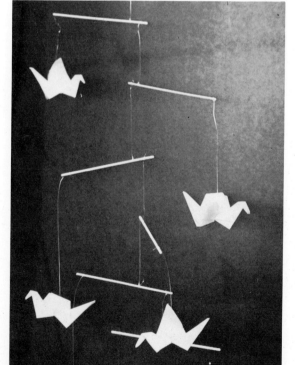

With nylon fishing line and wooden dowels, these light origami flapping birds continually fly about in space with only a slight breeze.

fold only comes into play when making the tail of the chimp.

Fold the arms back onto themselves as shown in Figure 4, to make them thinner. Again, keep a symmetry with respect to the center line of the original diamond as well as to the two sides of the monkey.

In Step 5 you break with the symmetry. Along the original diamond's axis of symmetry, fold the two identical sides of the monkey on top of each other. Make the creases shown in Diagram 5 in preparation for the folding of the head (Steps 6 and 7).

Fold as indicated, creating a front-facing diamond-shaped head (Step 6). Crease the head along the lines shown and fold so that the brow and the nose of the monkey will protrude slightly. To add the final touch to the chimp's upper half, fold the tips of the arms down so that the monkey has those characteristically dangling hands.

To make the lower portion of his body— the legs and tail—repeat through Step 3 in the making of the upper part of the body. At that point, ignore the two folds which make

the arms thin, but rather fold along the longer dotted line which cuts across the original basic form. (In other words, do the reverse of what you did in making the upper part of the body in Step 3). Fold down only one side flap from the top of the diamond as shown in Diagram 8.

Following the dotted lines in Diagram 8, make this folded-down triangle into a thin, pointed tail (Diagram 9). Fold down the tip of the as yet untouched remnant of the original basic form as shown in Diagram 10.

Along the axis of symmetry which runs through to the tip of the tail, fold the form onto itself, hiding all the tail-thinning folds on the inside.

To complete the feet and tail, fold these extremities as Diagrams 11 and 12 show— changing the angle of the tail, and putting the monkey flat on his feet.

All that remains of this monkey business is for you to attach the lower part of the monkey to the head and arms. With rubber cement, join them by gluing the lower half between the outer folds of the upper half.

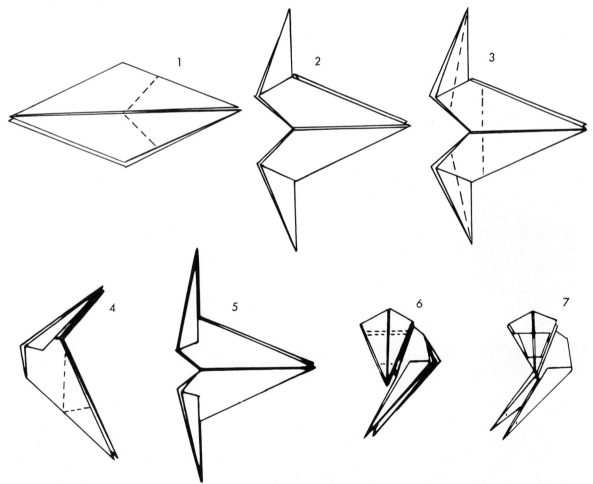

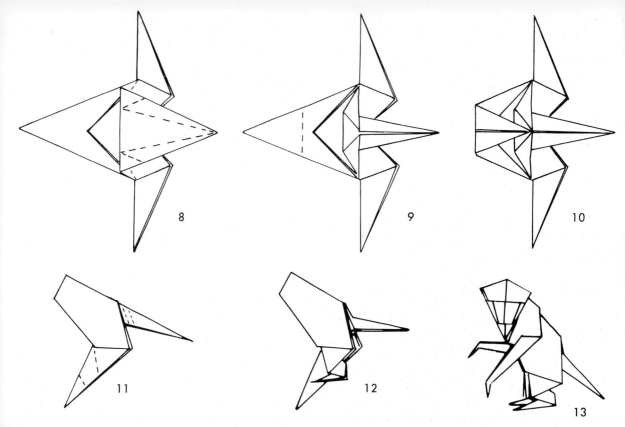

8

9

10

11

12

13

Apply rubber cement to the inside of the upper half of the monkey.

Insert the bottom half of the monkey inside the glue-coated upper half, thereby joining head and arms to the tail and feet.

If attached to thin extruded acrylic rods, you can have your own set of monkey bars.

Mask

Masks are used in all societies. In some cultures, masks fulfill important ceremonial functions; in others, they are used only occasionally at festive gatherings or by children.

The basic mask form shown here offers great potential. With the basic shape—an adjustable form that covers the head—many variations are possible. There are no rules for what the mask should look like, but design concepts do come into play. In this mask, for instance, the horns, nose, and upper lip were all formed from a single piece of white Scorasculpture that was added to the basic black mask form. The fewer pieces used in these constructions the stronger the mask will be—structurally and aesthetically.

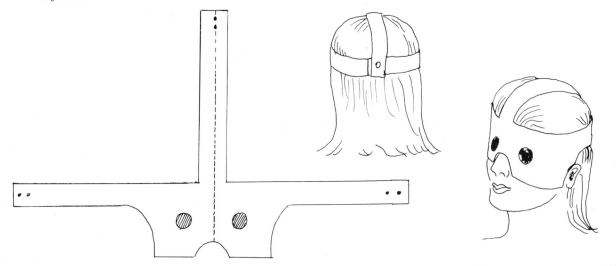

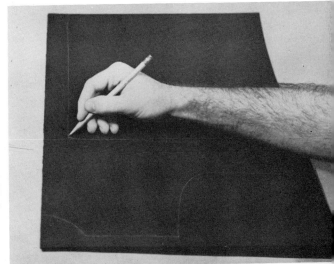

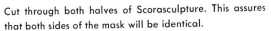

The basic mask form, onto which you build, is a simple, symmetrical piece of black Scorasculpture attached behind the head with paper fasteners.

Fold a piece of black Scorasculpture in half and draw half of the diagram on it. Be certain that the piece is large enough to fit around your head, and the dotted line in the diagram must correspond to the fold in the Scorasculpture.

Cut through both halves of Scorasculpture. This assures that both sides of the mask will be identical.

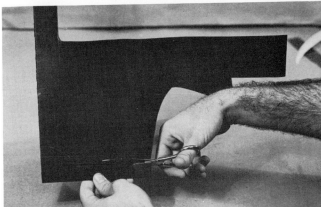

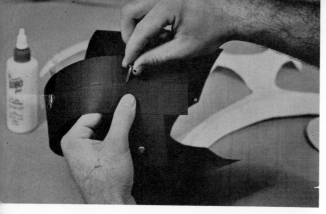

Test the size by fitting the mask around your head. Then attach the two side and one top strips together at the back with fasteners.

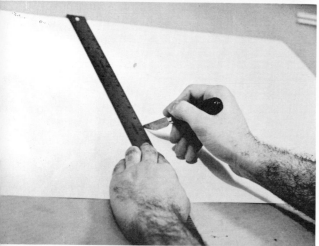

Build onto the basic black form with white Scorasculpture. The more additions you make with continuous pieces of Scorasculpture the more attractive the mask will be. And, unless your design in asymmetrical, it is a good idea to fold the Scorasculpture in half to ensure identical sides.

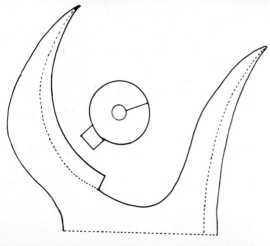

This mask will have horns, a large upper lip, and bulging, conical eyes. The dotted lines indicate what is to be scored and bent. Also shown here is the diagram for the lower lip.

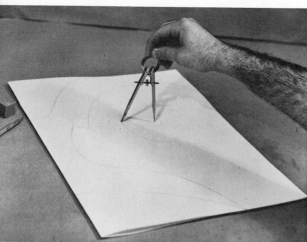

Translate the pattern onto a folded sheet of Scorasculpture making the eyes with a compass.

Cut out the form, and score with a scoring knife along the dotted lines. Bend along the score lines to add shape. Also, cut out the eyes, and include a small tab which will be used to attach the eyes to the mask.

Attach the "bridge" of the nose made with white Scorasculpture to this spot. Be certain that your vision will not be blocked. Hold the parts together with paper clips while the glue is drying.

Glue the upper lip to the bottom edge of the black mask so that the point of the lip (which doubles as the tip of the nose) protrudes. Glue the long and exaggerated sides of the lips to the sides of the mask, too.

Attach the point from which the horns begin to the forehead of the basic form. To facilitate this, you may want to make a small Scorasculpture tab and glue half of it to the back of the horns and the other half to the glue spot on the forehead.

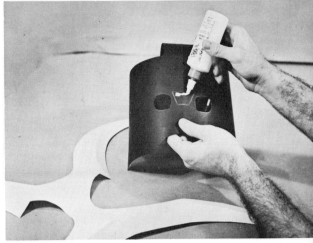

Apply white glue to an area between the two eye slits.

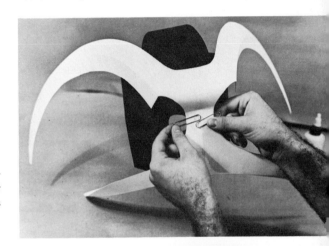

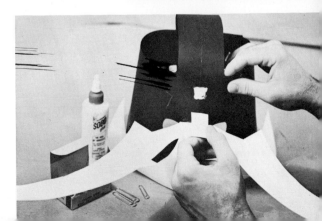

To make the eyes bulge, cut one straight slit through to the center. Now reattach the eyes with the slit edges overlapping one another, creating a cone shape.

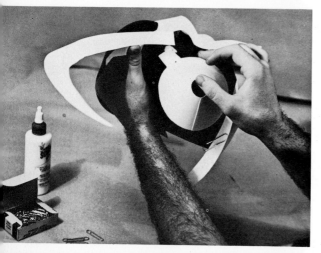

Attach the conical eyes to the black base mask by their small tab. Be certain, once again, that vision through the eye slits will not be blocked by these "false" eyes.

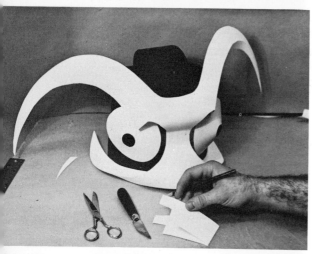

A small piece of Scorasculpture, scored and bent in the middle, will become the lower lip. The underside of the lip should be slightly longer than the top side. It is by this extra length that the lower lip is attached to the mask.

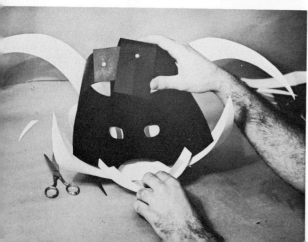

Glue the lower lip, by the longer tabs, to the mask. This lip should not interfere with putting on the mask.

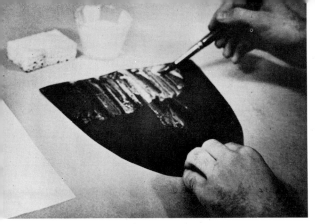

The chin for this monster was made with Scorasculpture decorated with glazed paper and felt paper.

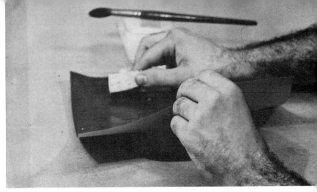

With a damp sponge press the glazed paper over the glue-coated Scorasculpture so that all wrinkles and air bubbles are removed. When all the edges are firmly bonded, trim away excess paper. The result is a chin with the strength of Scorasculpture and the color of the glazed paper.

A textural effect can be achieved by adding circles of Peel and Stick felt paper. Glue the chin to the mask behind the lower lip. The tongue is optional equipment.

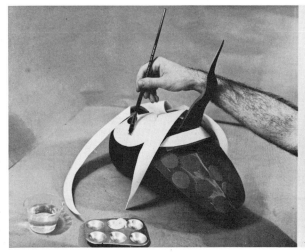

The horns, eyes, and lips may be painted with slightly thinned acrylic paint.

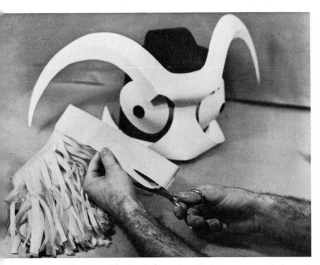

To make hair for this beast, deeply fringe several sheets of tissue paper. Attach this fringe to the mask behind the horns, and let it flow back to cover the black band on top of the wearer's head.

The completed mask.

Tubular Window Ornament

Groupings of tubes of various diameters and heights, some capped with tissue paper to filter the sun's light, others filled with decorative loops of paper, can brighten even an unwashed window.

To make a tubular window hanging, cut strips of thin, sturdy, colored or white cardboard to various widths—from 1″ to 5″. Using rubber cement, roll and glue each of these individual strips into tubes, varying the diameter.

Besides the cardboard strips made into cylinders, you may want to add color to the tube groupings with pieces of Artape, a craft paper with a gummed backing sold in rolls in 12 colors. This material can be cut to any length and is readily glued into tubular forms by wetting an end of the tape, overlapping, and adhering it to the other end. Any colored gummed paper can be used as well.

It is advised that when using the Artape in this window ornament you combine it with at least a few cardboard tubes, because these gummed papers themselves are rather thin and would not hold up well alone.

You can add light-coloring effects to the window ornament by tissue-papering the bottoms of some tubes. Cut a piece of translucent colored tissue paper to a slightly greater diameter than the tube end to be covered.

Apply glue to the cylinder's sides at one end of the tube, then carefully adhere the tissue paper to the glued surface. Make certain that the tissue paper has been stretched taut over the opening without tearing it or warping the tube's shape.

To cover up the unsightly crumpled tissue-paper ridge which now drapes over the outside of the bottom of the tube, take another piece of tube material of the same dimensions as the original tube and glue it over the original. This duplicate outer cylinder not only covers the messy glued fringe of tissue paper, but strengthens the tube form as well.

Artape can easily be bent and glued into the shape of a teardrop. Teardrops are glued together at some central point to look like the petals of a flower in outline. To add a new dimension of interest to the tubes, you could make several teardrops (or perhaps some gently spiraling scrolls) which would be glued inside some of the tubes.

Once all the tubes are made, arrange them and glue them together side by side. Leave spaces here and there and dispense or concentrate the tissue-paper cylinders throughout the design. Take advantage of different heights and diameters in distributing the colorful tubes.

String the cylinder decoration by one of the heavier top cardboard tubes. Hang it in front of a window. Now you can look at your handiwork in a different light.

After making tubes of assorted heights, diameters, and colors with thin cardboard and gummed-back Artape, fill some of the cylinders by covering their bottoms with tissue paper or by putting designs in gummed tape within them. A length of Artape can be licked along one end, doubled back over itself, and glued into a teardrop shape. A number of these teardrops grouped together as an internal design for a tube plays slicing tricks with light beams.

Attach groups of these tubes together and you will have an adornment for any window.

Corrugated Paper Swirls

Manufacturers throughout the world have long known the remarkable strength of corrugated paper as a boxmaking material and for displays. But this strength has applications outside of industry. Spiraling reliefs can be made of rolled corrugated paper strips. Thin strips of rolled corrugated paper butting against one another can form a handsome durable place mat or bas relief. And these are just two art-craft applications.

With a paper cutter or scissors, cut straight strips of corrugated paper. Tightly roll the strip with the ridged side facing out. Glue the end of the strip to itself, securing the roll.

If you are making a spiraling relief design, you will want to vary the length of the strips (hence, the diameter of the roll), the height of the strips, and the amount of spiraling.

To make a corrugated roll stand in relief, simply push out the inner rows of the roll from the underside.

If you are making a place mat, you will want to use very thin strips of corrugated paper of the same height. You may still vary the length of the strips, however.

To get the individual rolls to form an entire unit, just glue them side by side with an all-purpose white glue.

By pushing up from the bottom, these corrugated paper rolls can take on three-dimensional shapes. The texture can be quite exciting.

A place mat may be constructed with strips of corrugated paper of the same width.

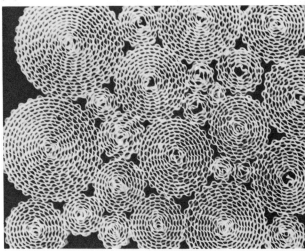

Roll strips of corrugated paper into tight cylinders with the ridges on the outside. Glue the end to secure the roll, and attach the roles with all-purpose white glue.

Rolls of corrugated paper were used in this section of a modular unit floor. The paper structures, which fill 5' squares 6" high are covered with glass. Courtesy: Container Corporation of America, and The Museum of Contemporary Crafts

Kites and Their History

In battle, religion, averting evil, and celebrating life, kites have had an important place in some Oriental cultures for as long as 3,000 years.

Two thousand years before the birth of Christ, religious observances of the Malayans called for kite flying. Flights of kites were recorded in Egyptian hieroglyphics more than 2,000 years ago. But despite these definite clues to the early presence of flying craft, China is thought by many to have been the pioneer in kite development.

Starting with sticks, large leaves of plants, and vines for cord, the kite evolved through the Orient to a high level of sophistication based on bamboo (and in heavy wind areas on cypress wood), paper, and cord.

There are legends in most Oriental cultures about battles which were influenced by and oftimes won through the use of far-flown kites. Around the beginning of the Christian era, during the Chinese Han Dynasty, kites, according to legend, caused troops of an invading army to flee in terror. They had been flown over the camp of the invading army one night with bamboo hummers attached. These kites sent out fearsome moans and screeches. As the legend goes, spies in the enemy camp passed word that these were gods declaring the defeat of the invaders, and thus the enemy was routed.

In other military activities, kites played a less dramatic but a more believable role as signals to troops—a kite raised at a palace could alert and call forth an army of defenders in short order.

Kites were also used in battle to airlift food to beseiged troops, carry messages to allies, and judge distances by the length of the kite cord. After the Middle Ages, kites ceased to be used as military aids. Many peacetime applications emerged.

A practical use of kites was made by Japanese architect Kawamura Zuiken, who lifted his workmen by kites to lay the tiles on the roof of the temple Zojo-ji, in the late 17th century.

Just a few decades later, an ingenious and daring Japanese thief named Kakinoki Kinsuke is said to have built a man-sized kite on which he flew to the roof of the dungeon of Nagoya Castle and stole the solid gold scales from high-perched dolphin ornaments.

Indeed, not only did the Japanese show great ingenuity in their use of kites, but they proved to be incredibly talented at designing improvements for high fliers. There are hundreds of kite designs, and many have distinct stories attached to them. Quite a number assumed special symbolic meanings.

Japanese folk hero Kintoki (said to have been raised by bears in the mountains, and who became the strongest man in Japan and an aide to the Emperor) is painted on Sagara kites which are given by friends and family to children as congratulatory gifts.

Kites decorated with a crane or turtle symbolize long life; the famed dragon kite denotes prosperity because of the dragon's ability to rise to the heavens; other kites are said to bring luck, scare off evil spirits, give hope for knowledge and learning, bring good crops, good fishing weather, and so on.

With all these meanings and legends attached to kites and kite flying, it is no wonder that these paper constructions became an integral part of many ancient and modern cultures.

In the Western world, kites came relatively late. They were well known in Greece's golden age around 400 B.C. And some scholars have speculated that the Cretan legend of Daedalus and his son Icarus (who flew too close to the sun on wax wings and perished) might well have been inspired by the stories of men flying aboard kites. Although present in Greek culture, as well as among the Egyptians, it is thought that the use of kites in the Mediterranean fell far short of the important role assumed by kites in the Orient. In fact, even in later years when use of kites spread to the rest of Europe and eventually to America, the adult eye was more often than not keyed to practical application rather than ceremonial, talisman, or simple fun reasons for kite flying.

Kites were used to tow boats home from

fishing areas. In 1825, an Englishman, George Pocock, invented his famed charvolant. This was a carriage which was drawn along the country roads by teams of kites. With the proper wind conditions, the kites towed horseless carriages at speeds up to 25 miles per hour.

Other Western applications include, of course, Ben Franklin's experiments with lightning, which resulted in his invention of the lightning rod; 18th- and 19th-century British meterological experiments in the higher atmosphere; and Wilbur and Orville Wright's kite experiments which led to towed gliders and culminated at Kitty Hawk in the first powered flight.

KITE BASICS

Materials for kite making have remained simple, changing little in the past three millenniums: light, flexible, resilient bamboo, cypress, or other wood, or plastic strips for the framework; an adhesive (the Japanese use a mixture of flour and water which is boiled until smooth, but all-purpose white glue or rubber cement gets the job done); thin, lightweight, strong paper, like the special Japanese kite paper which is available here, or even tissue papers; a thin string for binding the framework; a heavier string for flying the kite.

Some miscellaneous materials which will be useful for the kite maker are the ruler (kites must be made to precise measurements if they are to fly right); protractor (right angles are often essential); and paints, brushes, and scissors. Acrylic paints work well for decorating the paper if you add a few drops of water to thin the paint. If your paint is too thick, the paper may become rigid in spots, and may also lose its delicate and precise balance.

Modern kite makers keep an atomizer of water on hand so that after the painted paper face of the kite is attached to the framework, the small buckles and stresses in the surface can be eased with a light mist of water. As the water dries, the kite dries to a taut, even, smooth surface that will be better able to tolerate stress in high winds. Always paint your designs on the kite paper before mounting it on the framework. It is very difficult to paint neatly once the framework and paper have been glued together.

DIAMOND KITE

The most popular kite in North America today is the common diamond-shaped kite. Although this kite is large compared to most of those flown in the Far East, and is made with sticks of wood or plastic rather than the thinner small-kite bamboo, this American favorite is particularly simple in design and is a sturdy, high-flying type. Because of its size and shape, it is not as maneuverable as many smaller kites, but it will stand up to fairly high winds at great heights.

The kite framework is made of two sticks, one 36" long, and a crosspiece 28" long. Glue them together into a cross as diagrammed. Use all-purpose white glue at the joint. Be precise. Make certain that the sticks are joined at a point exactly halfway along the crosspiece. This becomes a fulcrum—a pivotal point—as in a weighing scale.

In addition to glue, you may want to reinforce the point of intersection with some lightweight cord.

With a sharp knife, make single slits at each end of the two pieces of wood. The guideline string around which the paper will be glued sits in these grooves.

With thin, sturdy string, tightly inserted in the grooves, complete the diamond outline of the kite as the dotted lines of the diagram indicate. Knot the two ends of the string together after making certain that the outline string is taut all around the form. The framework is now complete.

Cut a piece of paper so that it is the exact shape of the diamond framework, but with a 1" or 2" margin all around. This margin will be folded back over the string guideline and glued to the string and itself. Only at the points where the crosspieces stick out should the paper diamond conform to the exact size of the framework diamond.

Paint a design on one side of the paper with water-thinned acrylic paints. These paints dry very quickly.

When dry, line up the paper with the framework, creasing the margin of the paper to the exact size of the frame's string guidelines. Be certain the shorter crosspiece lies against the paper with the vertical strip behind it.

Now apply glue to these paper flaps, and carefully fold each flap over the string so that it adheres to the back of the paper, sealing the string between. Do this around the kite edge slowly, so that you make as few wrinkles as possible.

With string, join the two ends of the horizontal crosspiece. Pull it taut until the kite bows slightly and tie the string so that this tension remains. The stronger the wind the deeper the bow. But store the kite flat by untying the bowstring.

Allow the kite to dry completely. If you like, spray the back of the paper kite lightly with water from an atomizer to soften the wrinkles. Put the dampened kite in a place where it will dry evenly.

The diamond kite may be strung for flight in one of two ways. You may pass a string through to the front of the kite through a hole made at exactly the point where the crosspieces intersect. To make certain that this hole will not widen or rip in a wind, you can put loose-leaf hole reinforcers around the hole before threading the string (which is tied to the wood intersection) through the front.

An alternate method of stringing is to attach string to both ends of the longer vertical piece. Have these two pieces of string meet at a point which—looking at a profile of the kite—when held straight out is on a horizontal line with the horizontal wood stick.

The typical tail for this heavy kite is made of strips of cloth. Tear one long strip of light-weight fabric—about one and a half times the length of the vertical wood strip—and knot shorter strips of the same cloth at 5″ to 6″ intervals all along its length. Tie the tail to the base of the kite, knotting it around the wood stick of the framework, and hope for a brisk wind.

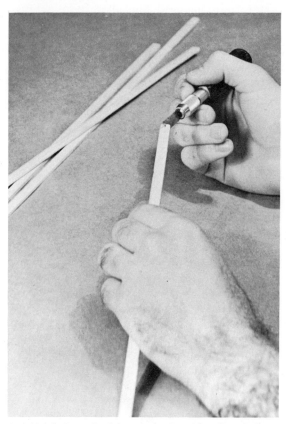

The longer vertical wood strip of the diamond kite is 36″ long. The shorter crosspiece is 28″. The dotted lines indicate the thin string which is slipped into the notches at the ends of the wooden strips. The string is pulled taut and serves as a guideline for gluing. The wood strips are adhered with all-purpose white glue, and the joint is secured with string.

Notch the ends of the wood strips with a sharp knife.

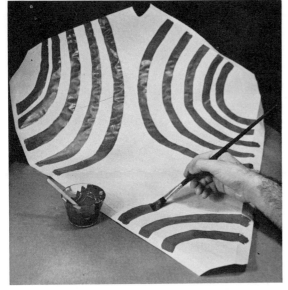

Use lightweight (but strong) paper which has been cut to the shape of the diamond—with an extra ½″ all the way around for gluing. Paint the paper with fast-drying acrylic paint (thin the paint first with a few drops of water). Paint that is too thick will make the paper inflexible and change its balance too much.

Affix a cloth tail to the base of the kite; bow the diamond kite according to the wind, and let her go.

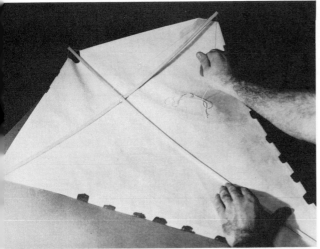

After gluing the margin of paper around the string guidelines you may eliminate wrinkles in the paper by spraying with water from an atomizer. Do not soak the paper, however. Let the water dry. To bow the kite tie a piece of string to both ends of the crosspiece; tighten the string until this is bowed. Use a deep bow for heavy winds, and release the bow entirely when the kite is not in use. Store the kite flat.

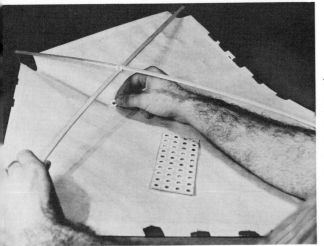

The kite may be strung for flying with one or two strings. In the two-string method one begins at each end of the vertical kite rib, connecting a foot or two in front of the kite on a line with the intersection of the ribs. The single string method requires that a hole be punched through the paper at the point where the ribs intersect. To keep this hole from enlarging secure it with loose leaf paper reinforcers. Pass the end of a roll of string from the front of the kite through the hole, and tie the string to the intersection.

RECTANGULAR KITE

This standard kite design is made with a more elaborate framework than the diamond. If you are using bamboo strips it is best to make the dimensions of the kite about one foot by one and a half feet. But if working with wood strips (which are not preferred for this design because of greater weight and less flexibility), the size should be about 24″ wide by 28″ long.

Construct the framework according to Diagram 1, using string and, if working with wood strips, all-purpose white glue.

The string guidelines along each side of the kite frame are attached by tying one end of the string to a corner where the horizontal and diagonal strips meet. Keeping the string taut, simply hook it once around the next rib's end. Repeat this for each successive rib until you reach the other corner of the kite where you again tie the string. Run the guideline string about one-half to one inch inside of the end of the shorter ribs so that the rib ends can stick out of the kite paper later on.

Repeat this process for the other side of the kite to complete the framework assembly.

If you are using wood strips for the frame, you will find that the multiple intersection at the center of the kite is rather thick and awkward. The thickness caused by four strips intersecting can be thinned by using a file. File the midpoint of the two diagonal strips so that just at the intersection they are about one third as thick as they were originally. Interlock the pieces, glue, and tie.

Cut out the paper for the kite in the shape shown in Diagram 2; add an additional margin for folding back and gluing. Also make holes at the appropriate points where the tips of the ribs will stick out.

Paint the paper with water-diluted acrylic paints or marking pens. Let it dry. Pass the rib ends through the holes, placing the two diagonal strips closest to the paper. Glue back the flaps with rubber cement or white paste or glue. Spray with a gentle mist of water from the atomizer to smooth wrinkles.

Stringing of the rectangular kite, as with all kites, must be done precisely and with great care so that the kite will fly well.

With a ruler, measure all sides to determine the exact center of the kite—you cannot trust your eye because the center might be fractionally off from the point of intersection of the strips. Make a hole in the paper at the true center. Also make holes at the two other intersections (marked by circles in Diagram 3). Attach lengths of string to the wood at these points, passing the string through the holes to the front of the kite. Attach string to the two top corners of the kite as also shown in Diagram 3.

These five cords should be brought together at a length at least equal to the height of the kite. But before knotting them together, the cords must be accurately lined up so that the kite will be balanced. As shown in Diagram 3, line up the five strings along the central vertical rib of the frame. But also, as illustrated in Diagram 4 (the side view of the kite), line up the five strings so that they are all taut at a point which lies in line with the second to the top horizontal rib. Make certain that all lines are taut; tie them together. Attach heavier cord to this juncture.

The reason for making the lines meet at a point which is not the geometric center of the kite is to allow the wind to get underneath, producing lift. On a normal flying day this is the best position for the strings. However, on windy days you will want some of the lifting wind to escape around the kite so that it is not lifted so strongly. To compensate for heavy wind, adjust the knotted group of strings so that they meet as lined up in Diagram 3, but a bit higher than the level shown (causing the flying kite to face more toward the ground).

The bow of this kite is important, too. Bow it with string connected between the two top corners and also between the two bottom corners. Again, use a heavy bow for heavy wind, a light bow for light wind, and release bow tension when not flying the kite.

The tail of this kite should be made of paper (Japanese or even crepe will do). Two tails of straight 2″ to 3″ wide paper should be attached to the bottom corners of the kite. The lengths should be equal and should be about three times the *diagonal* length of the kite.

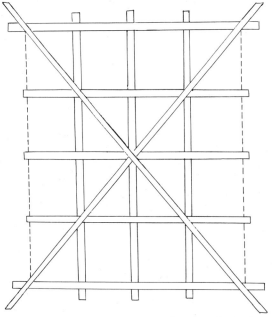

Diagram 1. If using bamboo for the frame, make this kite 12″ × 18″. If working with wood strips, the dimensions (due to the weight of the wood) should be approximately 24″ × 28″. Glue and tie the frame in this configuration. Dotted lines indicate the placement of guideline strings.

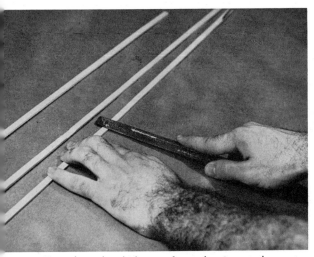

To reduce the thickness of wood strips at the center (where four strips must overlap) use a file to thin the middle of these ribs.

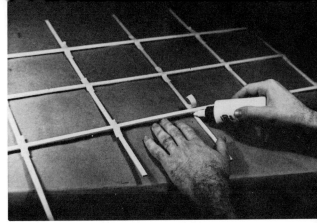

When working with bamboo, only string is necessary to attach the rib intersections. But, if working with wood strips, it is advisable to use a white glue, too. Apply the glue and hold the intersecting pieces together with strips of masking tape until the glue dries.

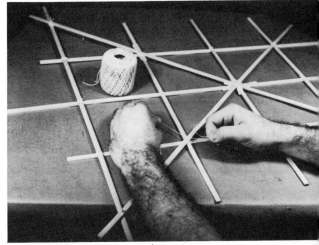

Now tie the joints with thin cord.

Having tied the wood or bamboo, run the guidelines from one end to the other as the diagram shows. Tie the string at one end, pull it taut, and loop it around the next rib. Continue to loop it around each rib, tying the string to the other corner. Repeat this for the other two corners of the kite frame.

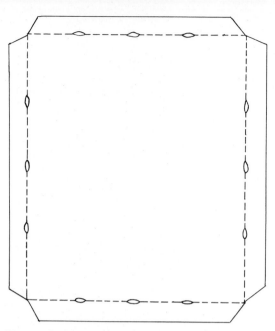

Diagram 2. Using a strong, thin paper, possibly Japanese, cut the shape of the kite, including an extra margin which will be glued back.

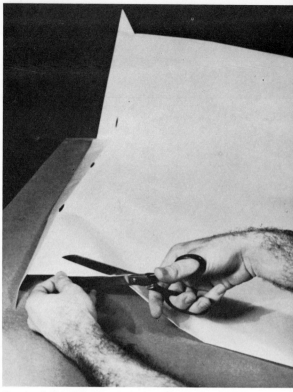

Cut the holes through which the ribs of the frame will protrude. Decorate the paper.

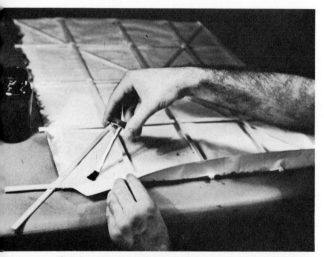

Slip the ribs through these holes, thereby mounting the paper on the frame with the diagonal ribs closest to the paper. Paste back the extra flaps of paper, minding the string guidelines.

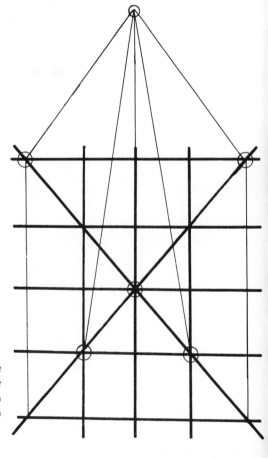

Diagram 3. The five strings, which will connect at a point as far from the kite as the kite is long, should begin at the circled intersections. The strings should come through the face of the kite, and they should line up tautly with the center vertical rib.

Diagram 4. When the kite is viewed from the side, the five strings should also meet on line with the horizontal rib which is next to the top one. This places the guide strings at an equal-stress point which is horizontally on center, yet vertically above center—permitting the wind to catch underneath the kite and give it lift and flight.

INDIAN FIGHTER KITE

Although there is a version of this kite made in most Far Eastern countries, varying according to the placement of the bent crosspiece, the Indian fighter kite is particularly outstanding not for its ability to fly quite high, but more for its controllability. The skilled kite-flier can actually direct his kite to swoop, attack, retreat, rise, fall—hence the fighter title.

This kite is best made of bamboo, which will accept a much greater bend than cypress or other wood strips. The bend is essential for making the fighter kite.

Take two lengths of bamboo kite strips 27″ and 21″. The 27″ piece will be bent and will become the crosspiece. The 21″ strip will serve as the vertical main mast.

Find the middle of the 27″ strip, and find a point a little more than ¾ of the way to the end of the 21″ strip. Connect the two strips at this point with string. Following the diagram, create a bend in the longer strip with guideline strings. Tie the cord to one end of the 27″ strip (it may hold better if you notch the end with a sharp knife). Keeping the string taut, wrap it twice around the end of the vertical strip (a notch will help here as well), then bring the string up to the other end of the 27″ strip. Pull the string until there is an equal bend created on both sides of the vertical line, then tie the guideline-bend cord to the end of the bent bamboo.

Notch the other end of the shorter bamboo strip (the one not bent) and run a guideline string from the end of the bent strip around this tip and back down to connect to the other end of the bent strip. This completes the frame.

A beautiful deviation from the normal cut-paint-paste formula for the kite face can be done with a very thin paper such as tissue paper.

Cut the sheet of tissue paper to a size a bit larger than the framework outline, so that you can fold back, and glue the excess. You may want to affix the paper temporarily to the framework with small pieces of tape at the corners. This may help you visualize the final product.

If you follow all these steps, you wouldn't be lion if you said you made this kite yourself.

With a sharp knife, cut out parts of the tissue paper. Then with another color tissue paper, cut pieces in exactly the same shape as those pieces removed—only make them ¼″ wider all around. With rubber cement, carefully paste these larger shapes over the holes created when you cut out the other forms. This kind of cutting and piecing reinforces the kite while functioning as a design. Fold and glue the extra edge of paper, following the guidelines.

Attach the kite's guide strings from the bottom tip of the vertical rib, and from the intersection of the two ribs. Use a loose-leaf paper reinforcer to help preserve the hole made in the tissue paper. Have the two strings meet at a point in line with the vertical rib and about an inch or two below the intersection of the ribs—well above the actual center of the kite.

Tails for this kite are folded widths of tissue paper slit many times (creating a fringe), gathered at an end, tied, and strung from the two ends of the bent bamboo strip.

Now get out there and fight. Go fly a kite.

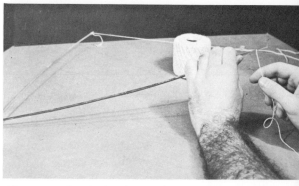

After connecting the bamboo at the intersection as diagrammed, attach the guidelines. Tie string to one end of the strip to be bent; wrap the string around the bottom tip of the vertical bamboo strip (this will create a slight bend). A small notch at the end of each strip will hold the string securely.

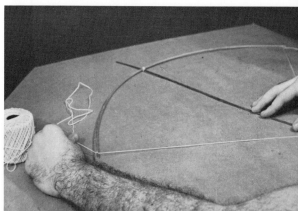

Continue to bring the string around; be certain that the bend in the crosspiece is symmetrical, and tie the string. Attach string along the top two lines as well.

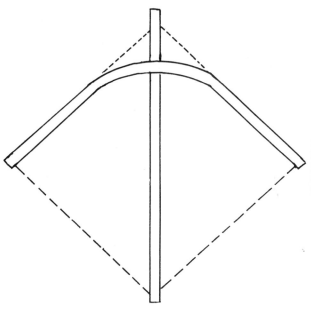

The Indian Fighter Kite is made up of two strips of bamboo—one strip bent and one strip straight—connected by guidelines.

Cut a piece of tissue paper slightly larger than this frame. Cut out designs with a sharp knife.

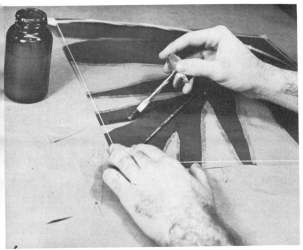

With tissue paper of different colors, cut out pieces that will fit over the designs you cut in the larger sheet. Paste these replacement papers over the cut out spaces with rubber cement. Glue the margins of tissue paper over the guidelines.

Attach tissue paper fringe tails to the ends of the bent bamboo strip. String the kite from the intersection of ribs and the bottom of the vertical rib.

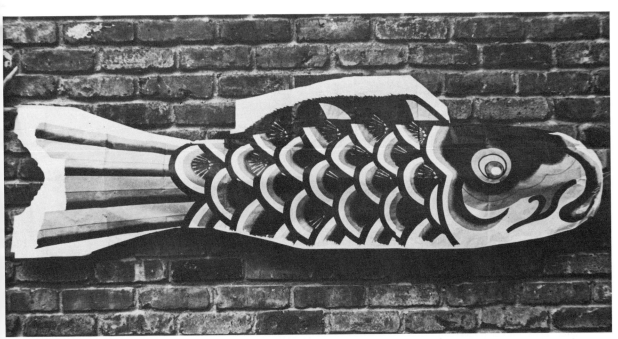

Although not a kite in the normal sense of lift and flying, this Japanese fish acts as a windsock and flies in the wind. It has a hole in the front through which wind passes, bloating the tubular form as the wind rushes out the open-ended tail. It is strung on a pole in front of Japanese homes to celebrate a male child on boys' day. If there are three male children in the family then there would be three fish.

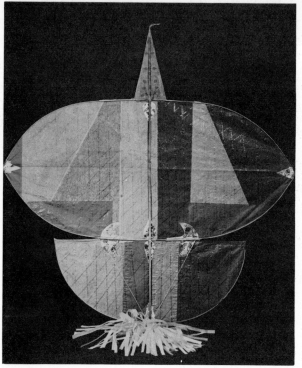

An Indian kite made of bamboo and patched tissue papers. The Indian kite makers use stuck-on metallic paper tabs to secure weaker and more heavily stressed points of the kite.

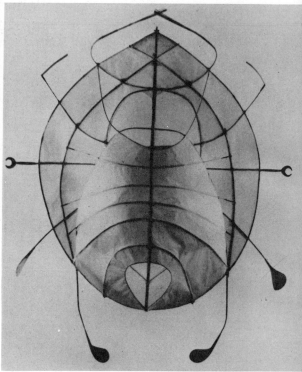

A bug kite sculpture, made in 1965 by Fumio Yoshimura of seki-sh paper on a bamboo frame, stands 39½″ × 32″ × 13½″. Courtes Container Corporation of America and The Museum of Conten porary Crafts

This classic Japanese centipede kite is made up of 11 circular Japanese paper components. Each is 10″ in diameter and the full kite extends to 6′. Because of its length it is also one of the more difficult kites to fly.

chapter 5

Sculptural and Architectural Forms

Three-dimensional forms with paper start with a piece of paper having four edges, two sides, and a basic consistency (hard, soft, and so on). Nature and geometry give us a vast potential in shape vocabulary. Paper provides other shape potential in tying, gluing, cutting, twisting, scoring, and bending. These can turn paper into whatever our perception decides. Shapes can be anything from found forms such as crumpled paper to invented shapes in three-dimensional geometric configurations. Nature ties in with the geometric. There is a mathematical order to nature; every natural form has an ordered composition: pinecone, snail shell, wave. But this geometry can bring us out of the realistic realm. With geometric underpinnings paper forms can be simplified, enlarged, combined, multiplied, and thereby transformed from flat pieces into exciting structures.

When designing for three dimensions we must ask what a piece of paper can do. Can it be stretched and shaped? What is its strength when folded, scored, curled? What joinings should be used—interlocking, gluing, taping? How can a particular volume be made? Can units be combined by grouping and stacking in progressions? What effects does light have in modulating the surface? What shapes are made in negative spaces?

After exploring the basic vocabulary of what paper can do and how it can be joined, new forms can be invented. One may employ papers in complex applications where the engineering of strength, stress, tension, and compression is important.

Papers will perform whether the conception is simple or complex. Paper prototypes are translatable into any material that can be formed and manipulated from a flat sheet. Paper may be an end product, but only in the sense that it expresses an idea. There is no such thing as a final form—sculptural and architectural forms are a continuum.

Straw Structures

White paper straws are a good material for beginning. Straws are regular units; they are readily available and easy to work with. Use string to make your straw structure. Suck the string through the straw. You will find that the basic building block of these structures is the triangle. Three straws tied together make a structurally stable form that can be combined very easily with more of the same shape. Large numbers of two-dimensional units can be used to define large tetrahedral forms.

Because the equilateral triangle is such a basic shape, many geometric possibilities are open. Also experiment with structures that are not regular. And experiment with different length straws as well. Before you begin to use different lengths, however, give your purpose some thought. Begin by varying just one side, and build some forms with this new triangle before introducing further variations. Once again, a systematic investigation will be the most rewarding.

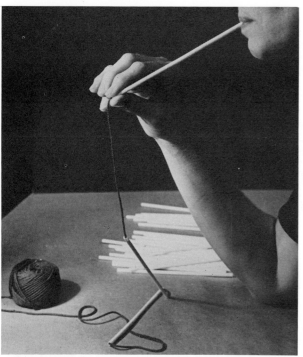

Paper straws can be connected by string. Suck the string through . . .

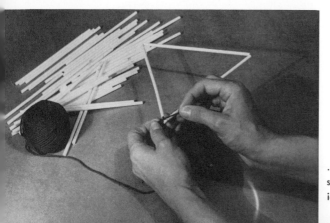

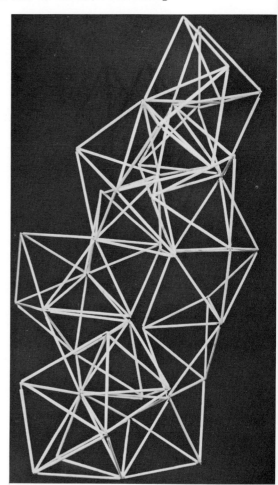

This form is 4' tall. Complex, dynamic forms are possible with this simple material. Also try varying the length of the straws.

. . . and tie off the straws in units of three. This creates a strong triangle which can be combined with many other identical units to make large structures.

Folded Paper Strip Constructions

Almost like erector sets, scored and folded thin paper strips can be used for imaginative constructions.

Begin by cutting dozens of long strips of a nonrigid board such as Scorasculpture. Make them all the same width—about one-half inch.

These cut strips are, of course, quite flimsy, but, by scoring each strip lengthwise down its center and then folding along the score line, these weak strips are converted into sturdy, erect, workable lengths of paper.

Use the strips in many ways. Realistic paper houses, and rhythmic, abstract constructions like the one shown here reflect the potential of folded strips.

This construction consists of pairs of vertical strips joined by series of shorter horizontal pieces that act as further reinforcement. Because of the network of long verticals and shorter, interlacing horizontals, this free-standing creation has a kind of syncopated rhythm.

With a ruler, mark off ½″ lengths of paper.

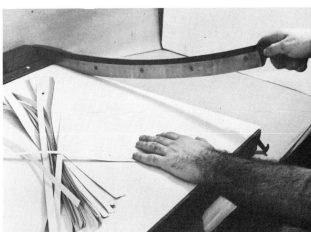

Cut several dozen of these strips with a paper cutter or scissors.

Using a ruler as a guide, lightly score each strip down its center.

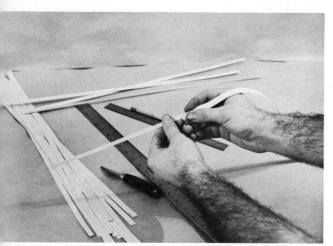

Fold the strip along the score line. This one fold will transform the strip from flimsy paper into an erect construction material.

To make a free-standing abstract construction with these paper strips, cut and adhere them with an all-purpose white glue.

This ladder-lattice was constructed entirely of thin paper.

A cut-paper tablecloth from San Andrés Huircolotla, Mexico.

Bowls and sculpture made with permanentized paper quilling.

A special technique combining handmade paper and leather, by artist Golda Lewis. *Courtesy, Golda Lewis.*

Papier-mâché vegetables from Mexico.

Two paper containers. One is woven, the other made of one large piece and a bottom.

A tissue paper collage.

Paper collage made with gummed colored papers.

Peacock Twirl, by Nell Znamierowski.
Ghiordes knots in corded paper yarn
over a warp of flat paper yarn.
Courtesy, Nell Znamierowski.

Building with Cardboard Strips

A high climbing staircase sculpture can be made from regularly shaped cardboard strips by a simple building process.

Cut strips of railroad board, Darby board, or another strong but flexible board. Glue the ends of the strip to each other, bending the board into a regular form: square, triangle, ellipse. The strips may all be of the same width and length or they may be gradually decreased in size so that the spiral will taper as it grows in height.

Stack these forms one on top of another, but twist each unit a little more clockwise— or counterclockwise—than the unit directly below it. To join the stacked units, make slits of uniform length in the top of each form so that the next unit will fit in properly.

Tall spiraling forms can be very appealing, but remember the limitations of the material. The taller the planned structure, the larger the base strips must be. The more secure the joints between strips are, the better.

A rising spiral construction has a special geometric appeal.

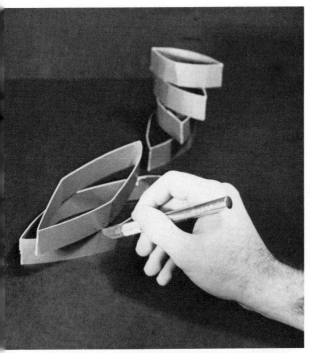

To build up the cardboard shapes in a progressively spiraling fashion, cut short, uniform slits in the top edge of each unit so that the next piece will fit in securely.

A view from above shows the symmetry of these forms.

Corrugated and Honeycomb Forms

Corrugated papers, used extensively in commercial applications for packaging and insulation, can be cut and shaped into exciting forms. Large blocks may be cut and sliced to reveal intricate, regular patterns. Still another technique is to twist and shape the flat, flexible honeycomb sheets manu-factured by the Union Camp Company. These honeycombed forms are generally manufactured in ½″ to 1″ thicknesses, but custom pieces can be made as well. Interesting optical effects are possible because the same sheet of honeycomb may be stretched and compressed in different sections simultaneously, resulting in variations of honeycomb spacing.

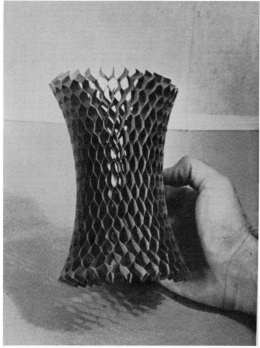

Because of its strength and design, honeycombed paper is an aesthetically and architecturally appealing material. This shows the effect of pinching Union Camp honeycomb at two ends. Uniform surfaces such as these tend to define geometric shapes.

Union Camp honeycomb can be twisted . . .

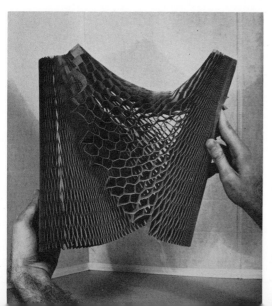

. . . and stretched . . .

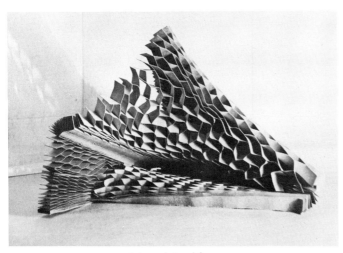

. . . into sculptural forms.

Untitled Sculpture, 1960, by Jan Peter Stern, is made of carved paper honeycomb. It is 27″ high × 30″ diameter. Courtesy: Container Corporation of America and The Museum of Contemporary Crafts

Expanded Paper

A close relative of the honeycomb is expanded paper. Paper is expanded by making row after row of parallel cuts. The cuts are staggered so that when the paper is pulled at both ends it will open—much like a honeycombed paper. This technique is particularly suited to experiments in density.

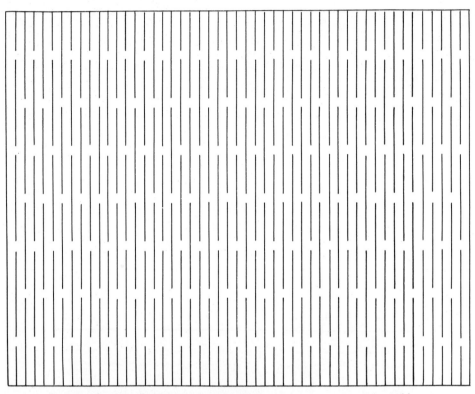

Paper can be expanded by cutting, with a sharp knife, in the pattern indicated here.

Use a straightedge, and be certain that your knife is sharp, because if the paper is not cut all the way through it will tear when pulled.

This technique is closely related to the honeycomb in the sense that the density of spaces can be controlled by varying the degree the paper is pulled. Spaces can be varied by cutting in different patterns, and the distances between cuts, and the cuts themselves, should be changed experimentally.

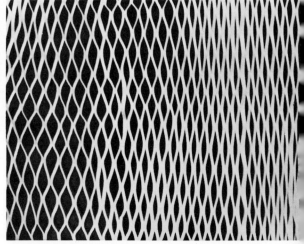

Tubular Forms

Tubular forms in paper may take many shapes. The most common are cylindrical and rectangular, but it is easy to visualize paper in any number of regular and irregular tube shapes.

The central concept in these structures is repetition of a design by slicing or piercing the tube. Continuity of design from all views need not mean the repetition of identical units of design, but rather that the patterns follow some progression or common denominator.

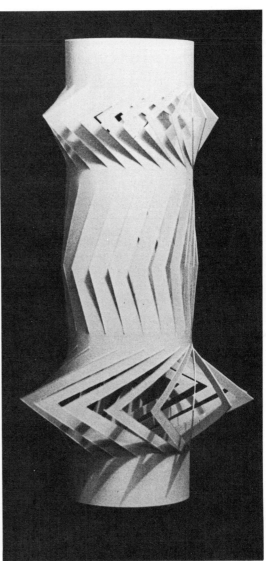

A single piece of Scorasculpture was cut in three bands of parallel shapes, bent, and attached to create this design.

This rectangular tubular form was constructed by folding along each corner, cutting and scoring each section alternately, and attaching the Scorasculpture's ends so that a single, boxlike piece resulted.

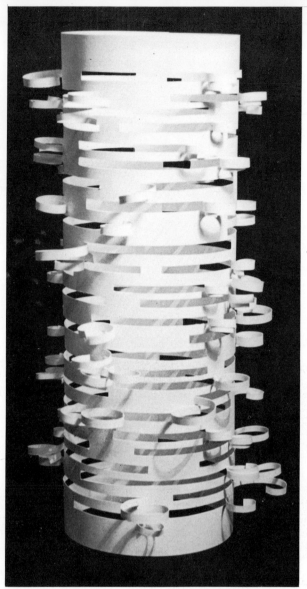

Thin strips were cut and curled from a single sheet of Scorasculpture in this example. This form is the same as . . .

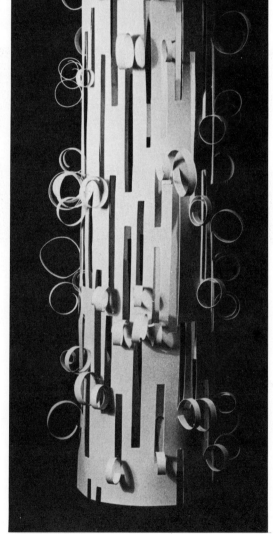

. . . this one, but the paper was bent in a different direction in each. Both effects are striking.

Light Modulators

Moholy-Nagy described every piece of paper, crumpled or bent, as a light modulator. That is to say, the paper catches, reflects, and modulates light in a way that other flat surfaces cannot. A flat surface will only reflect light.

Light modulators may be made out of other materials besides paper, but because papers are so plastic they offer the best modulating possibilities.

Modulators need not be complex. A long strip of paper curled and twisted around and around offers many bends and twists on which to catch, reflect, and modulate light. Other modulators can be cut and twisted from single sheets, or they may be made with forms that have been scored and combined. Piercing a surface with a hole introduces a void that interrupts light and becomes a darkness.

In no sense should the notion of a light modulator be considered a definition or a requirement of a form. Rather, it is a description. Most three-dimensional forms modulate light simply by virtue of being three-dimensional; this descriptive term gives expression to an important aspect of our analysis and appreciation of sculptural surfaces. What we see is determined by light, and by controlling our surfaces we can orchestrate light's effects.

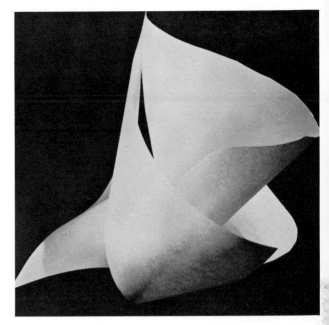

Or modulators can be cut and shaped. These two pieces were each constructed from a single piece of Scorasculpture that was cut, twisted, and pinched.

Light modulators can be as simple as the strip of Scorasculpture that was bent, twsited, and attached at its ends.

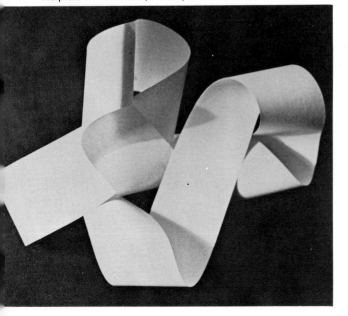

Scored forms can act as modulators as well. In fact, all curved surfaces modulate light. A spiral of Scorasculpture was scored down its center in this example.

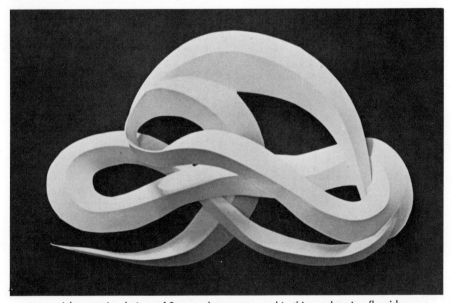

A large twisted piece of Scorasculpture was used in this overlapping flourish.

Scored Forms

Curved scored forms can also act as light modulators. And scoring is a technique that is adaptable to modular and repeat units as well. Because great precision is possible with scored and bent surfaces, this technique lends itself very well to the creation of modular units. Curved modules, linear modules, and integrally modular pieces are possible.

Because precision is often necessary where scored units work together, accuracy is important. Plan scored lines by lightly penciling them in on the paper. Measure accurately, and make certain that the angles are correct. You will discover that some materials are better than others for this purpose. Scorasculpture, by Dennison, is manufactured specifically for this purpose. It is extremely well suited for scoring, and it is available in white, black, and silver and gold metallic.

A single module in metallic Scorasculpture looks like this, and it may be combined with other modules . . .

. . . to construct larger forms. Courtesy: Dennison Manufacturing Company

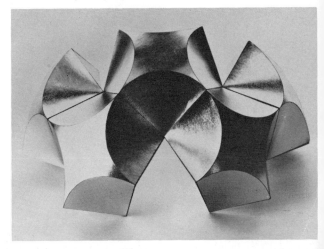

Polyhedral Inversions

There are a number of regular geometric forms that can be constructed, by scoring and folding, in such a way that they revolve around a central axis.

Although the sizes and patterns of these forms vary, they are all made up of triangular units, either isosceles or equilateral. The form shown here is made up of isosceles triangles which rotate around a circular axis to reveal different configurations of the constituent triangles.

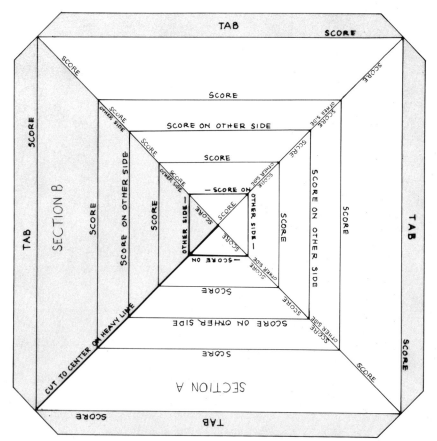

A 10″ square of Scorasculpture is used here. Score the indicated lines. Accurate scoring is essential in a geometric form like this. Start in the center and work out. Be certain to score on the proper side. Cut to the center on the heavy line and glue section A securely over section B. Courtesy: Dennison Manufacturing Company

Because the units are equilateral triangles they fit together securely in the shape of a regular hexagon. Courtesy: Dennison Manufacturing Company

This plaque illustrates the superb scoring and folding properties which Scorasculpture offers. The triangular design gives it a number of faces to catch and reflect light.

Pleated Forms

Pleating greatly increases the strength of paper, and striking results can be achieved by folding and refolding pleated papers. Because this type of structure imparts great strength to the material, it is employed in a variety of applications with as many different materials. Corrugation, which is the same principle, is used on metal sheets, and concrete structures use a similar technique for added strength. The most familiar paper structures using this process are lamps, which have enjoyed long popularity.

The accompanying photographs show two methods of effectively folding pleated papers. One employs a process by which the direction of the pleat is alternated for each fold. This demands that the angle of the fold be determined beforehand. The other method utilizes an additional "lip" of paper which is folded before pleating. The angle can then be determined afterwards by pulling and creasing.

When pleating papers, be certain to choose a paper that is easily folded and refolded (unless you intend to achieve the same result by scoring all the lines). A fairly thin, flexible paper works best, since the pleating will increase the dimensional stability of the paper. Just as the strength of the thin scallop shell is increased because of its folds, you need not worry about further supports.

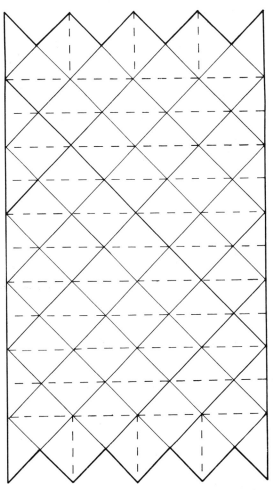

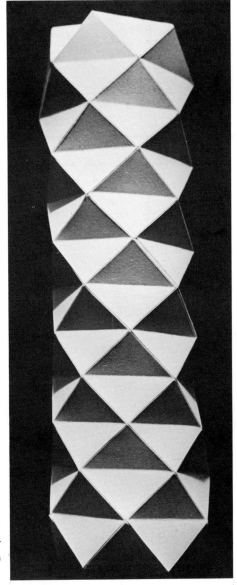

The solid and dotted lines in this diagram indicate that the Scorasculpture should be scored on opposite sides.

The result is a closed, architecturally powerful tower composed of isosceles triangles. The form is closed with paper tabs and adhesive.

Once again, the different lines indicate scoring on opposite sides. Be certain that all lines are accurately measured.

This piece, also composed entirely of isosceles triangles, has quite a different effect.

This spatial structure, by Kurt Londonberg, was made of scored and folded paper. It is a 25″ cube. Courtesy: Container Corporation of America and The Museum of Contemporary Crafts

These two 12″ cubes of score-folded paper strips glued at their joints were also designed by Kurt Londonberg. Courtesy: Container Corporation of America and The Museum of Contemporary Crafts

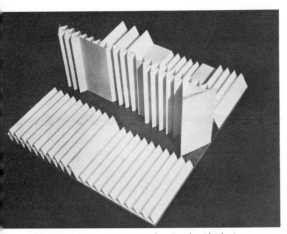

Boxed Monuments, 1969, by Cecile Abish, is a paper construction for Multiples. Courtesy: Multiples Gallery

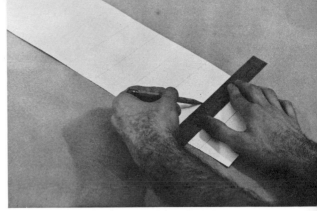

Begin by lightly marking the Scorasculpture in the proportions indicated in the diagram. The Scorasculpture, not including the tabs at one end, is four units wide by twelve units long. Be certain to leave some extra paper on one end for the tabs that will come later.

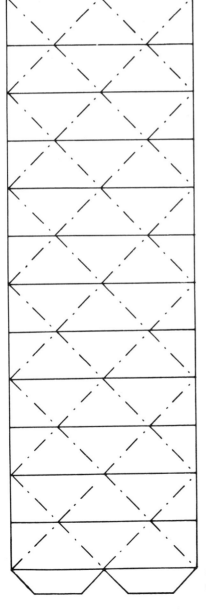

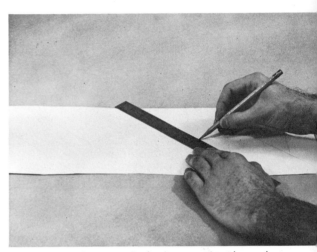

After marking the perpendicular lines on one side, mark the diagonals on the other.

In this diagram the solid lines are to be scored on one side; the dot-dashed lines are to be scored on the other side.

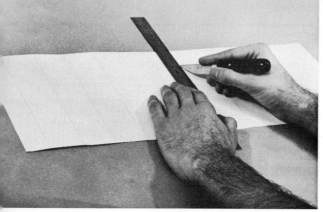

Use a knife to score all the lines accurately. This is crucial.

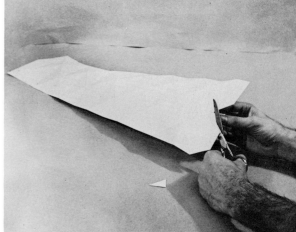

From the extra paper, cut two tabs at one end as shown.

Firmly bend along all scored lines.

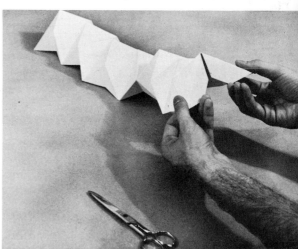

The paper should now look roughly like this when pressed together. Now grasp the tabs and pull them together until they . . .

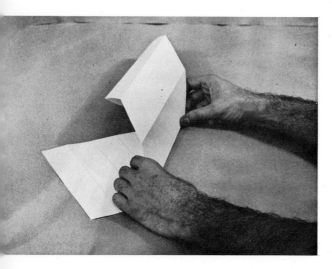

. . . form a square as shown here. The next step is to gather the Scorasculpture in successive squares.

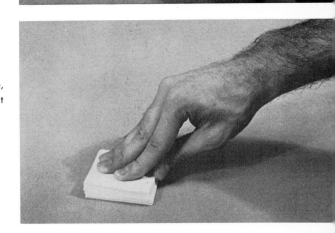

Still holding the top square, use your other fingers to draw in the rest of the paper. It should pleat easily.

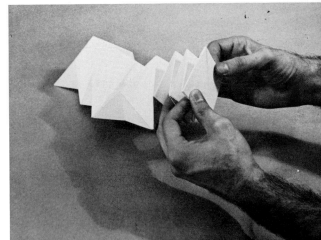

When you have gathered the paper into a solid square, press it down firmly on a solid surface, and hold it in that position for several minutes.

Release the paper and spread it out again. One side will be slightly convex. That is the side to decorate. In this example, plastic adhesive films were used, but you could use paints, inks, or other papers.

Once more fold the paper into the squares, and bend this accordion around (with the open edges on the inside) until the ends come together. Use rubber cement to attach the tabs underneath the corresponding triangles.

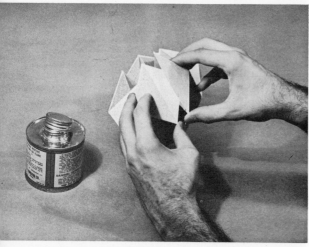

One tab will attach at the top and the other at the bottom. The form is then complete.

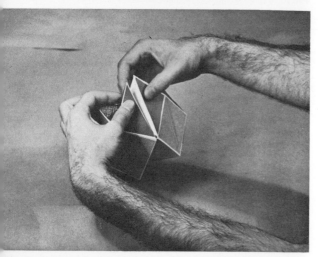

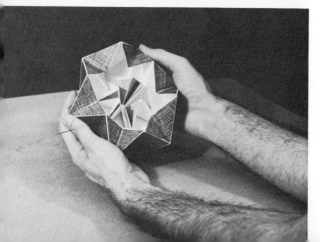

The form is now ready to be rotated around its axis. To do this, twist inward (or outward) with both hands. Do not force the Scorasculpture. It will move in and out easily. If any creases pop out of place, simply push them back.

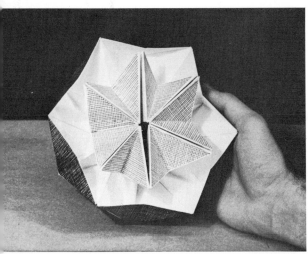

These three photographs show a progression as the surfaces are rotated outward from the center.

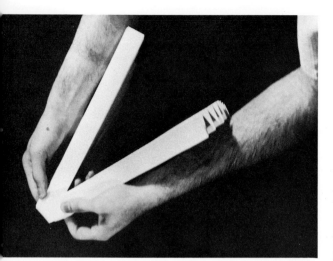

The first step in pleating is to fold a sheet of paper into a series of pleats of the same size. With a thin paper this may be done by continually folding the paper in half. Thicker papers will require the use of a ruler, and some may need to be scored. For most purposes, pleated forms should be made with a thinner paper. The first fold we show here is begun by bending a pleated sheet and making as sharp a crease as possible along the line of the fold.

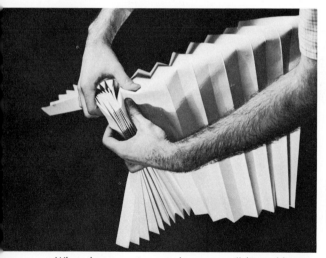

When the paper is opened, creases will be visible in a zigzag across the entire width of the pleated paper. Follow the creases. The pleats on one side of this fold will have to be creased in the reverse of their original direction as you move along the paper. Gather the paper as you move along.

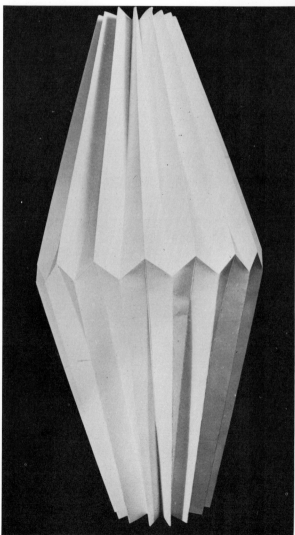

After the fold has been made, the paper may be spread like this. Only one fold was made here.

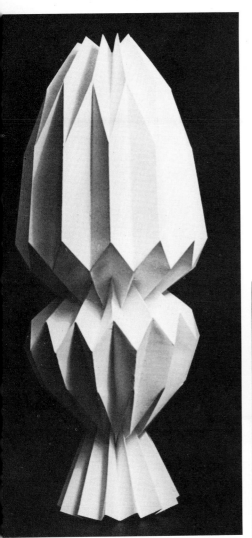

Other possibilities are offered by making several folds in the same piece. Remember that the original crease determines the angle of the fold.

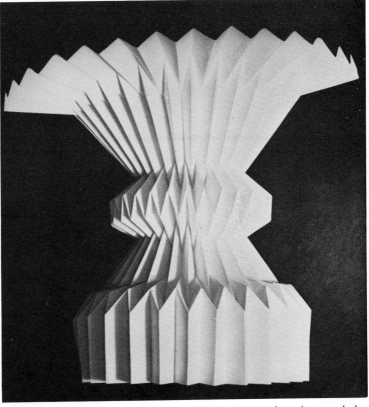

This form is actually the same piece as the one in the preceding photograph, but it was spread in the opposite direction.

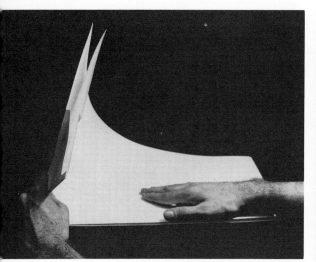

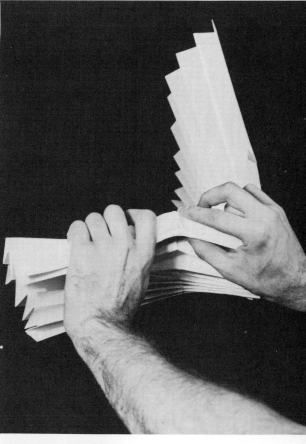

There is another way of folding as well. Before pleating, make "lips" by folding up and then folding back the paper. Then pleat the paper.

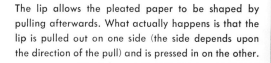

The lip allows the pleated paper to be shaped by pulling afterwards. What actually happens is that the lip is pulled out on one side (the side depends upon the direction of the pull) and is pressed in on the other.

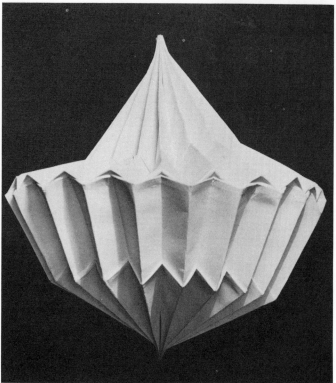

The form that results will perform the same functions as the forms constructed with the first technique.

Sculptural shapes may be made with this technique as well. This form, using gold metallic Scorasculpture, was made by scoring the paper, since this material is not readily bent and creased by hand.

This form, made of black Scorasculpture, is an example of the exciting shapes that are possible with multiple folds. The ends were attached with rubber cement.

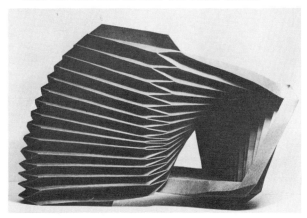

Bas-Relief Modules

Large, handsome structures can be constructed with squares, triangles, circles, or any other regular shapes as the basic units. First make a pattern, and cut notches in each shape at regular intervals. In the case of the square, notches were cut in two places: in some units at the corners (on a diagonal), and in others in the middle of each side (and parallel to the sides). In circles the possible locations for notches are increased—and units of different shapes can often be combined if their sizes are compatible.

Another idea, using a similar technique, is to use shapes of graduated sizes to define a space. In the example shown here, 11 squares were cut in ½" graduations, notched in two places each, and fitted together to create a cube defined by three planes of concentric squares.

Begin by making a pattern out of heavy paperboard.

Squares notched on their sides were combined in this structure.

Use the pattern to cut further shapes, and cut notches in the sides or corners with a knife or scissors. Bristol board was used in these structures because it was stiff enough to allow for larger forms.

The units should fit together easily.

In these, corner notches were used.

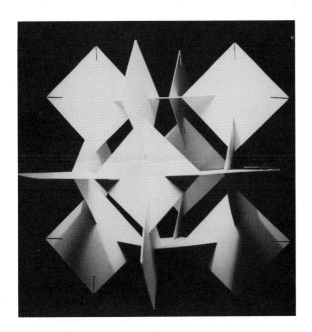

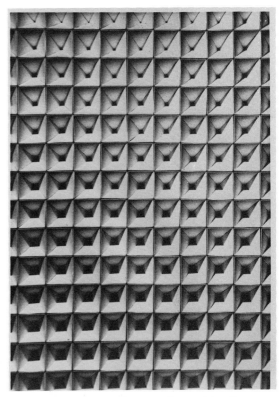

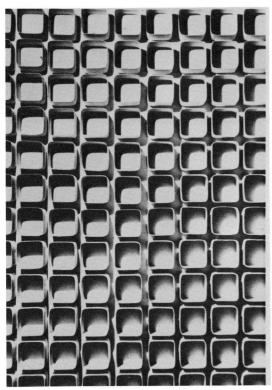

These two paper units are also part of a modular floor unit concept and double as wall panels. Courtesy: Container Corporation of America, and The Museum of Contemporary Crafts

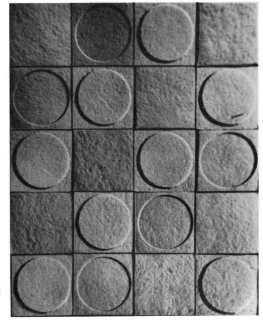

These modular wall tiles were press-formed from handmade paper. Designer: Hiroshi Minamizawa. Courtesy: Container Corporation of America, and The Museum of Contemporary Crafts

Architectural Forms

In the last twenty years a number of architectural forms have been created using paper. R. Buckminster Fuller used the triangle as his basic unit and created a series of geodesic structures for which he has earned renown. But more recently, an entirely new series of paper possibilities has emerged. These designs, by architect/designer/engineer Ernest R. Schaefer, use several different modular units in the construction of domes made of paper. Schaefer's domes are quite remarkable in several ways. They are extremely strong, as stress analyses have proved; the units often require no adhesives, but fit together perfectly, and his forms are clean and beautiful as well.

Good architectural design should meet three criteria: it should be concise, economical, and efficient. By concise we mean that it should be based on essentials like mathematical relationships between materials and terrain.

Paper is a material that can be prefabricated and then erected to form geometric structures that are models for larger forms. With the aid of a computer, standardized forms, modern production techniques, and plastic impregnating materials, we can create domes to span great spaces while resisting compression and tension. By applying mathematical principles to modern techniques and materials we can vault large areas with a minimum of material and expense.

Because paper can itself be used in structures of large size, and because paper can be used to experiment with processes commonly used with other materials, it is the most practical vehicle for prototypes.

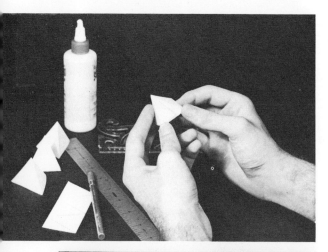

Each of the equilateral pyramids used here was made from a flat strip of paper. Each strip should be measured, marked, and scored in the pattern of four and a half continuous equilateral triangles. The half triangle will be used as a tab to glue the unit together. Use white glue or rubber cement.

The three planes here are made up of eleven squares graduated at ½″ intervals. They fit together with notches on two sides.

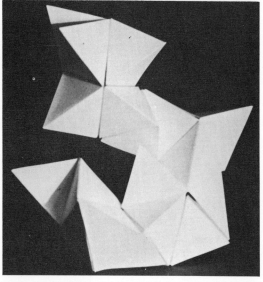

Twenty-five pyramids were combined in this architectural form.

This pattern describes a basic geodesic dome. The tab fits into slits.

The completed structure, composed of 20 equilateral triangles, looks like this.

The geodesic concept was invented by R. Buckminster Fuller. This geodesic dome was constructed in 1953 of Yale Cardboard. The diameter is 30'. Courtesy: R. Buckminster Fuller

A later dome (1959) shows a variation on the original structure. The diameter of this structure is 19', and it is built of Monsanto Chemical foam-core paperboard. The outside surface is coated with a urethane for protection from the elements. Courtesy: R. Buckminster Fuller

This scored and folded foam-core playhouse/toolshed is a testament to paper's strength and durability. The ½"
board was painted with an oil-based paint, and the structure has withstood ten years outdoors. Courtesy: Ernest R.
Schaefer

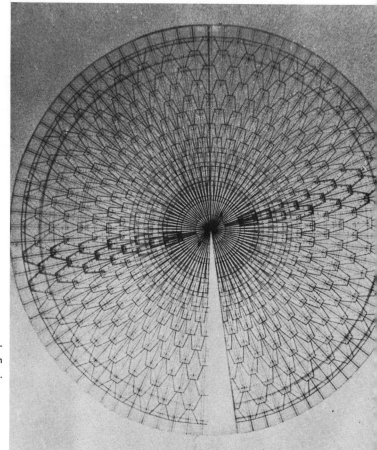

Ernest R. Schaefer designed this structure, Dome #2, for construction in
paper, plastic, steel, or aluminum.
Courtesy: Ernest R. Schaefer

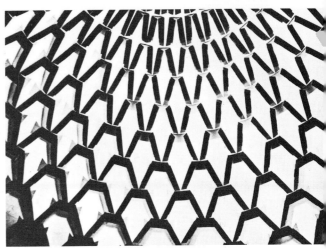

The basic units for Dome #2 are shown here in scored and folded fiberboard. Courtesy: Ernest A. Schaefer

In each unit of Dome #2 the height and depth are the same; only the width varies. Courtesy: Ernest R. Schaefer

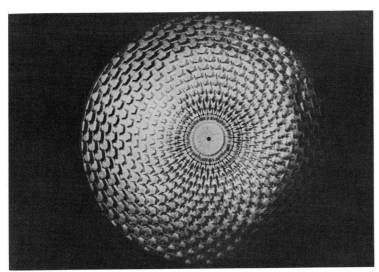

The units used in the construction of Dome #2, which was originally presented by Schaefer in a paper at Yale University, have also been adapted, using laminated paper ⅝" thick, to form a structure that will span 250 feet and withstand 150 mph winds and a snow load. Courtesy: Ernest R. Schaefer

Because the units fit inside one another, the entire dome can be packed in 18 boxes for easy shipment. Erection of the dome is quick and easy, too. Courtesy: Ernest R. Schaefer

Dome #3 was designed by Schaefer as an acoustical building unit. Every unit is made of wax-coated fiberboard cut to the same pattern. This dome will support steel rods (they fit through the slits in the fiberboard) while concrete is sprayed over the dome. The outside is then smooth, and when the dome is removed from the inside of the structure an acoustical surface remains in molded concrete. Courtesy: Ernest R. Schaefer

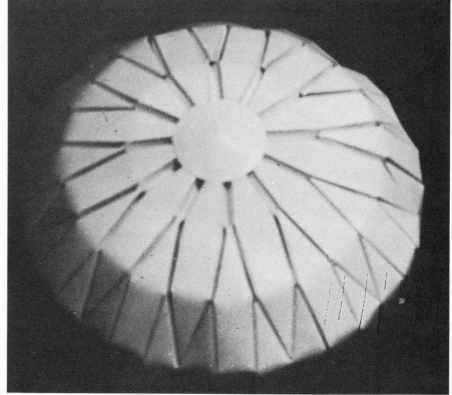

Schaefer's Dome #4 is constructed of scored and folded fiberboard held together with hardware inside the dome. Courtesy: Ernest R. Schaefer

Dome #6 is constructed of loops of paperboard cut in two patterns. Courtesy: Ernest R. Schaefer

This structure is adaptable to paper, plastic, steel and aluminum. The original model, of course, was a paper construction. Courtesy: Ernest R. Schaefer

A full side view of Dome #6 designed by Ernest R. Schaefer. Courtesy: Ernest R. Schaefer

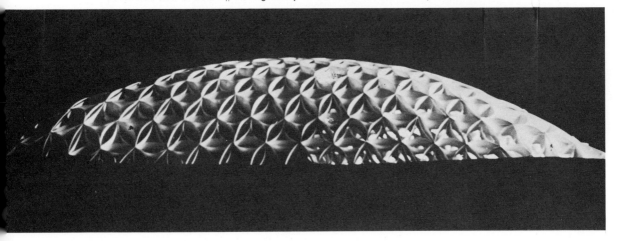

chapter 6

Collage

The art of collage, before its use by Picasso and Schwitters, for centuries was adopted by uninhibited folk who were less skilled in painting, and by primitives. Although recognized today as a "legitimate" art form, the departure into collage by professional artists began only in the early 20th century.

For years artists had been concerned with more or less photographic representations of real world images. They followed strict traditions for the proper and pure use of paints. Tradition was binding, and so, even though paper had been used as a background for watercolor and printing for as long as oil paint, the incorporation of paper textures and materials into the work itself remained a taboo and was avoided.

In the revolution that marked the emergence of "modern art" in the late 19th and early 20th centuries, artists began defying tradition by mixing media in the interest of expression. The photographic image—best achieved by the camera—liberated artists like Cézanne, Picasso, Schwitters, and Braque. With this liberation, the incorporation of found objects—beginning with pieces of paper—into art objects began.

No longer insecure about having to display their prowess as artists along traditional lines, the Cubists, and later the Dadaists, Futurists, and Surrealists were free to turn toward collage and its offshoot, assemblage (the art of combining three-dimensional found objects). The idea was to use the

This scene of "Christ Carrying the Cross," made in South Germany in 1750, is a folk art collage, combining cut silk and paper with a watercolor drawing. 146 mm. × 188 mm. Courtesy: Cooper-Hewitt Museum of Design, Smithsonian Institution

WEST'S *Theatrical* PORTRAITS.
Nº 55.

J. C. KEMBLE, *as* PRINCE *of* WALES.
In the Coronation, as Performed
at the Theatre Royal, Covent Garden.

Watercolor tinsel trimming and satin brocade embellish an engraving after West of "Mr. Kemble as Prince of Wales." This theatrical dress design, done in England in 1821, is another example of the collage's ancestor.

object, rather than to represent it by painting it. So the collage technique of composing a work of art by combining materials which would not normally be associated with one another found broad acceptance as a form of creative expression. Newspaper clippings, theatre tickets, wallpaper, and envelope fragments were a few of the materials of the early collages.

Pablo Picasso was among the first to employ "found" papers and combine them with paint on canvas. He would paste on pieces of paper for their color, texture, pattern, and planes. But such "junk" was not always in service of some other subject on the canvas, but could represent itself as well. Although for the Cubists paper pasted into a collage could symbolize objects, it more often was meant as a way of including pure and special textures in the art.

How the materials fitted into the planes, shapes, shades, textures, and hues of the work was usually the central and most exciting purpose of "junk" in art. The natural or real meaning of a piece of paper had its place, of course, as the later exponents of assemblage demonstrated. But for the initia-

tors among the Cubists—Picasso, Braque, Gris, and Schwitters—there was a fresh interrelation of shapes, lines, geometrics which could be rhythmically organized into a newer, more spontaneous shorthand for expression.

Kurt Schwitters, who fathered much of the collage-assemblage direction of today, is the prime example of what it means to rescue random, unrelated urban junk objects from the garbage can and create a kind of order in art expression. Besides paper, Schwitters combined many other materials and even art forms themselves into a new personal medium called *Merz*. His use of collage and assemblage ranged from early paper and paint on canvas to *Merz* drawings, which were small collages, to three *Merzbaue*, which were art forms but were also actual houses constructed with found objects.

The Dadaists and Surrealists also adopted collage and assemblage as another mode of shocking people by using real materials in unexpected and unintended ways.

Collage as a medium is as valid today as it was in the early 20th century.

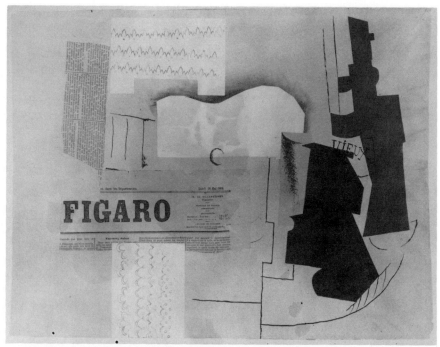

Guitar, Glass and Bottle, by Pablo Picasso. This collage example is typical of the early uses of cut paper, such as newspaper, combined with paint and other materials. For a while, Juan Gris, Picasso, and Georges Braque did similar collage work. Courtesy: The Tate Gallery, London

L'escargot (1953), by Henri Matisse. Cut paper collage. Courtesy: The Tate Gallery, London

Collage with Squares Arranged According to the Law of Chance (1916–17), by Jean (Hans) Arp. Pasted papers. 19⅛″ × 13⅝″. Courtesy: The Museum of Modern Art, New York

Merz 458 (1920–22), by Kurt Schwitters. This one of Schwitters's collages is a composite of streetcar tickets, wrappers, ration stamps, colored paper, etc. 7″ × 5⅝″. Courtesy: The Museum of Modern Art, New York

Tissue Paper Collage

Thin, translucent, colorful tissue paper is an excellent collage medium, and can be readily controlled on a cardboard background.

Besides the dozens of colors available, new colors can be worked into a collage by overlapping sheets and running colors together. Most of the dyes used in tissue papers are not colorfast, and so, when gluing the tissue paper to a cardboard background, the color flows and mixes. By overlapping tissue colors such as yellow and blue, or red and blue, the tissue combination will result in greenish or purplish hues, respectively.

Tissue paper can also be cut and folded. The folding intensifies the basic color, makes the paper more opaque, and often adds a touch of line geometry to the design.

Glue the tissue paper with a mixture of 50 percent white glue and 50 percent water. Acrylic emulsion can be used in place of white glue.

There are many other ways of working with tissue paper besides plain collage. Using the same gluing technique, for instance, you can make posters, silhouettes, decorations, stained-glass effects, greeting cards, murals, and use tissue paper as a final covering over papier-mâché.

In three dimensions, tissue paper can be used in conjunction with a chicken wire base. Bend the wire mesh into the desired shape as you would form a sculpture armature. Brush a vinyl wallpaper paste such as Metylan on the chicken wire. Then stick 6″ squares of tissue paper into every other hole of the chicken wire, leaving the edges sticking out. This ruffled, feathery covering becomes the surface of a solid-looking sculpture. The form can be very colorful.

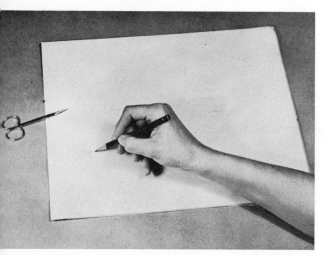

Draw a design on the tissue paper sheets for the beginning of a tissue paper collage.

Cut with scissors.

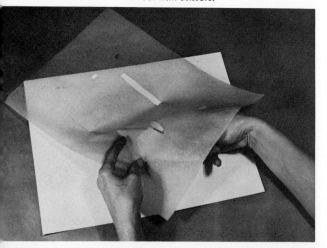

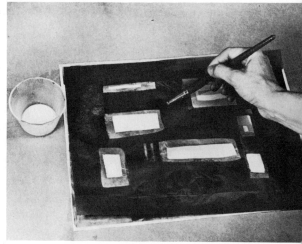

After cutting all the sheets, apply them to a heavy cardboard backing with a 50% water, 50% white glue solution. In this design the lightest color tissue papers were applied first.

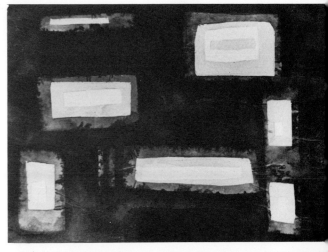

Since most tissue papers are not colorfast, the water-glue solution will cause some degree of bleeding and mixing. This can be used to your advantage as in this handsome tissue paper collage. (The subtle and varied colors do not show up in this black and white photograph.)

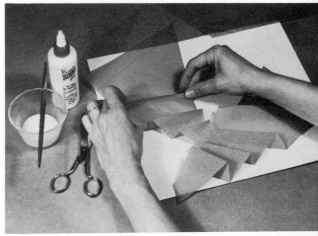

The tissue paper can also be folded and then glued down. Arrange the folds.

Apply some glue to the background with a brush.

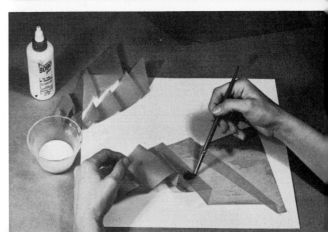

Place the folded tissue paper, and assure complete bonding by coating the top of the tissue with more glue.

Do the same for the rest of the design.

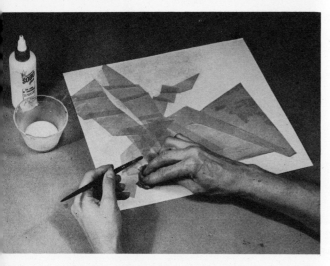

With a soft cloth or paper toweling, mop up any excess glue. Here the toweling is also being used to spread the bleeding color around the rest of the background.

Folding and gluing down the folds add a new dimension of opaqueness, line, and movement.

Tissue paper collages made from torn paper.

Instead of torn tissue, these cut strips have an almost Futurist look of motion.

The transparent tissue paper colors overlap in this design. Some of the colors bleed.

Paper Collage Paintings

Jane Bearman "paints" with special papers that she colors herself. Beginning with a large sheet of paper, she wets down the sheet on a wooden board and colors it with watercolors and occasional splashes of India ink. When the paper dries slightly, she removes it from the board and places it over newspaper to dry. The paper is sprayed with an acrylic fixative when fully dry.

From these colored papers, Jane Bearman cuts forms and adheres them to prepared canvas with a white glue. The colors do not run because the papers are protected by the fixative. When all pieces are in place, she paints the canvas with an acrylic medium to protect the surface.

Jane Bearman uses many different kinds of paper. Some have embedments of wood chips or fibers, others are clear and smooth. The first step is to wet the sheet down on a wooden board with water applied by brush or sponge.

The wet sheet is then painted with watercolors. If the paper begins to dry while painting, be certain to wet it down again.

Another effect Jane Bearman uses is to flick India ink onto the paper. The ink will spread at different rates depending upon how wet the paper is.

Different colors and shapes are combined on canvas. Carefully cut and plan the shapes first. Jane Bearman used white glue to attach the papers to a prepared canvas.

Remove the partially dry paper from the board and place it on newspaper to dry completely. When fully dry, spray the paper with a fixative.

These collage paintings by Jane Bearman use a background of darker paper to accentuate the lighter forms.

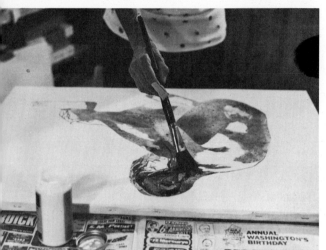

The finished canvas is painted with an acrylic medium to protect the surface.

Nude Think, by Jane Bearman, is a paper collage painting.

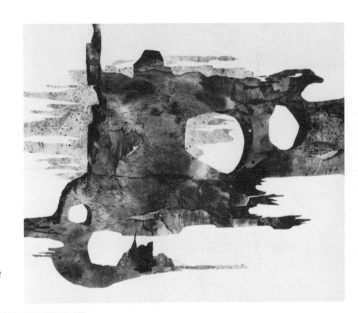

Jane Bearman's fantasy formations float eerily across the canvas.

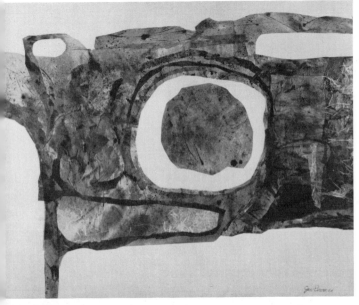

Nine, by Jane Bearman, contains nine figures or forms.

The Musicians, by Jane Bearman.

This dramatic tissue collage by Virginia R. Osterland incorporates the techniques of cutting, tearing, overlapping, and bleeding.

Sandwiched Collage

Clear photograph mounting paper, when heated with an iron, will adhere to other papers, sealing flat objects in a paper sandwich.

Lay out a pile of newspaper. Cover the wad with waxed paper. On this background, place a piece of light-colored construction paper, bristol board, or Scorasculpture. If you want to make a sealed fern collage the front of a greeting card, fold the sheet of paper in half like a card.

On the folded card, lay out dried ferns, or perhaps some colored paper pattern of your own choosing. Cut to size a piece of photograph mounting paper and place it over the dried fern design.

Cover the whole with another piece of waxed paper. Run an iron, which has been set for a low heat and no steam, over the waxed paper which covers the mounting paper and card. Don't worry about the wax which melts onto the iron. Press down and heat all parts of the card for as long as it takes to adhere the mounting paper to the card (30 seconds to a minute).

Let the piece cool and then remove the top sheet of waxed paper (you may have to cut it away if the outer edges of the two sheets of waxed paper fuse together). Trim the excess photograph mounting paper around the edge of the card.

When the design is complete, cover the ferns and background paper with a sheet of photographic mounting paper. Start heating your iron to a low temperature, no steam. Cover the mounting paper with another piece of waxed paper.

Lay out dried ferns on a piece of heavy paper. The paper is set on a bed of newspaper which is covered with waxed paper.

Run the heated iron over the sandwiched design, until the mounting paper adheres completely to the fern's background.

Let the papers cool, then remove the waxed paper and trim away excess mounting paper. If you place the ferns on a folded piece of background paper, you can make greeting cards.

Dried ferns sandwiched between heavy paper and photographic mounting paper.

Torn tissue paper as well as other papers can be combined in the sandwich under the mounting paper.

Quilted Paper Collage

This unique concept in paper collage uses threads and sewing for attachment. Stitches become an integral part of the design. Decorative papers are combined and temporarily glued into a pattern with rubber cement. They can then be sewn together on a sewing machine. Decorative patterns and stitches may be used.

Paper insulation material or other soft thickness of paper such as tissues can be used as wadding in between papers in the collage to add relief and a soft, padded, quilt-like feel. (See the Regal quilted rug in Chapter 9.)

To make a paper quilt, lay out cut decorative papers and temporarily glue them together with rubber cement. Paper insulation or wadded tissues can be used underneath the decorative papers as padding for the quilted look.

Sew the papers together along their edges.

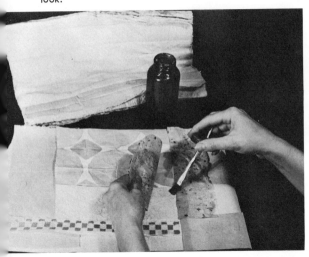

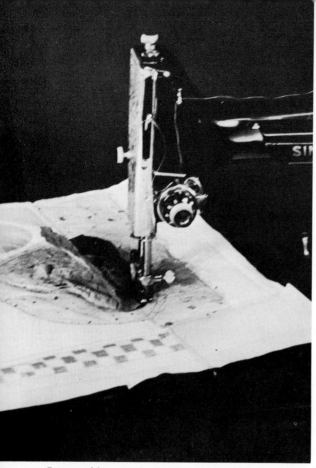

Extra padding can be slipped under a second layer of decorative paper.

The stitching is an integral part of the paper quilt. Special stitches can add variety.

Compage

Compages by Golda Lewis are collage-assemblage and a very personal form of expression. These compages are made of, not on, paper. At first, Golda Lewis made paper in the traditional way on a screen as described in Chapter 1. As her process became more sophisticated, she developed mixtures using a sizing that would permit her handmade paper to adhere directly to raw linen canvas and to the assemblage of scrap pieces that became an integral part of the composition.

The canvas becomes the paper mold. Some areas of paper are white, others are in colors which are at once intense and subtle. The textures are gorgeous, yielding a rich impasto of mat fibers.

Different colors are added to areas, sometimes with acrylic paint filling sections and providing accents. Impasto permits overlapping of areas of handmade paper and collage in a shallow relief.

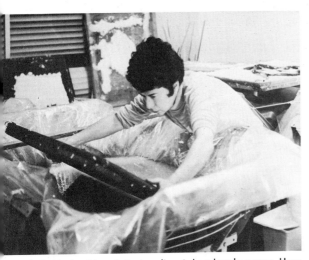

Golda Lewis's painting medium is handmade paper. Here she is dipping her screen frame into a suspension of cotton and linen fibers.

Golda Lewis lifts her frame out of the tub. Note that other found objects were placed on the screen as well. She often incorporates fascinating scraps of metal, leather, wood, and so on.

She stirs the fibers in preparation for another dipping. But some fibers may be lifted out in a fistful and deposited in particular areas of her "compage" (collage-assemblage).

The screen is allowed to drain until most of the water falls away. A sizing is placed in the fiber-water suspension so that particles adhere.

Sometimes Golda Lewis makes a whole sheet as she is doing here.

She is going to release a whole sheet from her frame onto a felt-covered curved table.

The paper is released from the frame and is allowed to dry between felts.

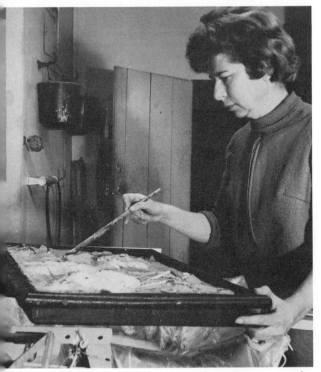

Sometimes Golda Lewis applies acrylic paint to areas for accents. The entire process is flexible, permitting many deviations from the standard methods of papermaking (see Chapter I).

A compage by Golda Lewis is rich and exciting in texture. Her "relief paintings" are made of rather than on paper.

Golda Lewis's "AG 47-1970" is 34" × 26". In this piece "raw" paper was made directly on raw linen canvas with the inclusion of rusted metal, wire, and strips of metal. The paper merges with and is absorbed by the canvas.

Another compage by Golda Lewis employing a variety of collage materials along with handmade paper.

To quote from the catalog of Golda Lewis's 1970 exhibit in Denmark, "A rag becomes a brush stroke. Wood chips, scuffed leather, bits of jewellike debris are organically integrated into figure and ground." This compage is "BF 22-1969" and is 26" × 22".

Collage of Printed Matter

While at the turn of the century railway tickets and newspaper clippings may have been the readily available, hence readily used, collage materials, today's innovations in color printing have opened the pages of innumerable magazines to the scissors-in-hand collage maker.

Comedy, crisis, con jobs, and all the other elements which form the contents of today's periodicals can be clipped, arranged, and pasted in a legitimate collage tradition of found materials.

Savage, by Carl Federer, is a collage made of magazine clippings.

Earth 2 (1962), by Leo Manso, is a collage of painted fabric and paper on cardboard, 23″ × 20″. Courtesy: The Museum of Modern Art, New York

Carl Federer's *Feather Fury* is made of colored strips cut from magazines and other printed sources.

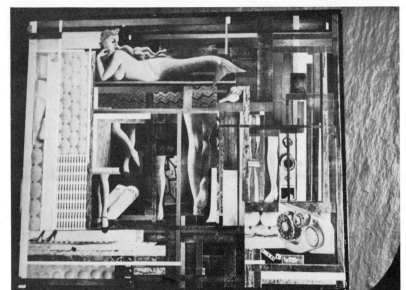

Wistful Mermaid, by Carl Federer is also composed of pictorial elements.

A true collage of found paper materials, Dorothy Cole's creation was built from picture postcards, magazines, advertisements, photographs.

Maria (1958), by William Getman. Torn paper posters on masonite, 47¼" × 35¼". Courtesy: Mr. and Mrs. Eddie Albert

Marisol's seated creations are made of wood, fabric, and paper. Courtesy: Sidney Janis Gallery, New York

Three-Dimensional Collage

By making an open-topped box or using a ready-made box, compartmentalizing it, and filling the compartments with different treatments of paper, you can create unique, highly textured, three-dimensional collage.

Crumpled tissue paper, confetti-like strips of paper, bent strips, curled scrolls, tubes, "transparent" Japanese papers—these are a few objects used to fill or cover a cavity.

In order to avoid turning the collage into a mix-up of papers, however, repeat some of the treatments in the design, watch for the distribution of lights and darks and qualities of textures such as soft, hard, angular, smooth.

By applying paper to boxes and stacking them into a construction, Barbara Schwartz made a three-dimensional collage with a theme.

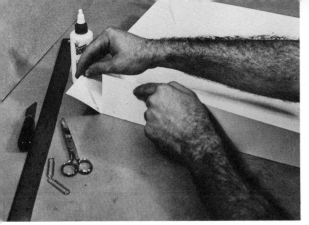

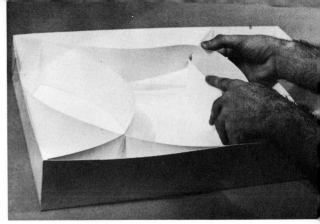

Make an open-top box out of oaktag or railroad board by scoring at a prescribed depth around all four edges, folding up the sides, and gluing the corner flaps together.

Insert equally deep strips of oaktag in the box to compartmentalize the three-dimensional collage.

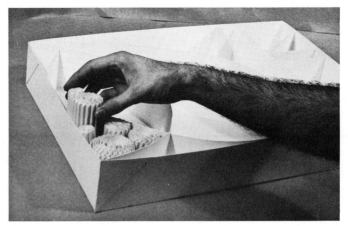

Fill the box with paper treatments such as rolls of corrugated paper.

Other treatments include folded construction paper, curled paper scrolls, strips of tissue paper, heavily curled thin strips of two-colored paper, crumpled paper, cut and painted cardboard rolls placed over a background of glazed paper, and special Japanese paper which covers the tops of two of the compartments.

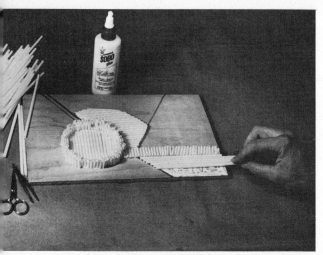

On a piece of plywood or chipboard, glue paper straws in different arrangements. Some may be cut and stood on end, others may be laid horizontally, vertically, diagonally.

Straw Collage

Paper drinking straws can be arranged and glued to a plywood backing to form yet another type of collage—this time in shallow relief.

By standing straws on end, on their sides, vertically, horizontally, diagonally, interesting textural effects can be achieved even with this pedestrian paper product.

Use a white glue on the straws. Tweezers may help you place the smaller cut pieces. You may also want to try coloring the straws or combining them in a collage with other paper materials and colors. One possibility might be to apply tissue paper under, over, and around the straws. This would add a curious, colorful, textural effect to the collage.

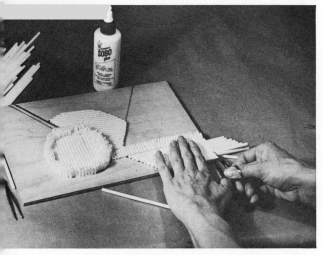

Cut off extra lengths of straw with a sharp scissors.

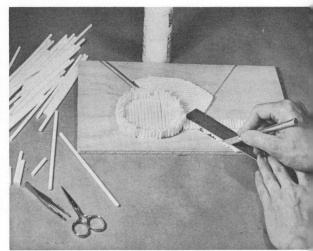

Using a ruler as a straightedge guide, cut off the uneven edges of groups of straws with a sharp knife.

A drinking straw collage in shallow relief.

chapter 7

Decoupage and Papier Mâché

Decoupage and papier-mâché are both old paper arts. Decoupage dates back to the 17th century when Venetian furniture makers tried to simulate Chinese lacquerware. From there it spread throughout western Europe, and, as it spread, interpretations of the technique changed it in each country.

The Chinese inventors of paper had an edge on exploration of the paper arts. Papier-mâché's beginnings are credited to the Chinese. Later, the Persians and Japanese used it mainly to create masks and other festival forms. From the Far East and Middle East papier-mâché spread throughout the world. Unlike decoupage, papier-mâché found continual application, probably because it is a structural material from which small forms, like containers, or large objects, like stage sets, can be made. Decoupage, on the other hand, is a means of decorating and finishing an object—sometimes made of papier-mâché.

Decoupage

Decoupage is a French word meaning "a cutting out." Traditionally, decoupage involved precise cutting of paper, usually from engravings or other prints, that was hand colored, glued to an object, varnished with many coats, and sanded until the edges disappeared under the many layers of varnish.

A BIT OF HISTORY

At first decoupage attempted to imitate Chinese lacquerware for people who could

A 17th century Italian decoupage writing chest using elements of hand-colored prints and hand-painting on a gesso background. Courtesy: Museo Civico, Padova, Italy

A close-up of the writing chest.

A modern version of a chinoiserie style of decoupage by Gini Merrill.

not afford the expensive original versions. The imitations were done over gesso-coated cheap wood. The gesso hid imperfections. When reproductions were used in Chinoiserie themes and styles, hand painting was eliminated, making furniture even cheaper. People began to appreciate the art for its own sake and soon Chinoiserie subject matter gave way to prints by François Boucher and Jean Antoine Watteau.

After the Victorian era, decoupage disappeared as an art until Caroline Duer Maybelle and her son, Hiram Manning, and Carl Federer revived the art in the early 20th century. Decoupage has been variously interpreted by its many disciples from traditional designs that imitate 17th and 18th century styles to variations on the theme by contemporary exponents.

THE DECOUPAGE MODE

Decoupage is an applied art using flat pieces of paper to decorate three-dimensional forms. Scissors hand-tailor printed or cut paper designs to suit the style and contours of the object. The form can vary and be made of almost any hard material: wood, metal, ceramic, fiberglass, acrylic, glass. Clocks, boxes, purses, cabinets, doors, screens, and panels are but a few possible objects that lend themselves to decoupaging.

Edges of shapes are usually hard or crisp because that is the way scissors cut. The paper is adhered flat or in relief on the object with an adhesive such as Elmer's glue. When dry, the entire piece is coated with many layers of a transparent varnish, one of many plastics available. When at least five to eight coats of varnish have been applied, depending upon the thickness of the paper decoration, the entire form is sanded, more varnish is applied, and more sanding is done, until the edges of the paper disappear into the varnish and one can no longer feel the perimeters of the paper shapes. At this point, paper, design, and object, through glue and varnish, are an integral whole. The shape of the form and its decoration have become one.

Decoupage is not difficult to do, but it does require meticulous attention to detail. Varnishing takes time and cannot be hurried. Paper needs to be cut precisely. With a mastery of the simple skills involved in this process, anyone can achieve a creditable result. Decoupage has the potential to be highly personal inasmuch as one's own way of seeing decorations and combining them produces a long-lasting and precious result.

THE DECOUPAGE PROCESS

No drawing skills are necessary in decoupage. One can find colored or uncolored prints in books, magazines, posters, and greeting cards, and illustrations are produced especially for decoupage. A fine quality, thin paper stock is best; it takes less varnish to cover. Uncolored prints can be colored with oil based pencils, watercolors, or transparent acrylic paint. Start with lightest colors first and work toward the darkest colors. Black or brown printing ink works best as an outliner for uncolored prints. Limit the colors to just a few. This usually works best.

After coloring the print, and before cutting it out, spray the print with an acrylic spray such as Krylon or Blair; use two light coats. This prevents the colors from running later on, keeps aniline dyes from bleeding, and strengthens the paper while sealing the surface.

Measure the print before cutting by comparing it to the surface it will lie on. Study both size and shape and consider how they will relate to the position and design of the print. Look for unusual possibilities and consider combining elements from several different prints.

Prints must be cut precisely. A fine, steel, small-curve-bladed scissors that resembles a cuticle scissors is used. Scissors like these permit greater precision than cutting with a knife.

Scissors are held with the thumb and third (middle) fingers in a relaxed position, with the curved blade pointing to the right and away from the edge being cut. Feed the paper into the middle of the scissors blades. Open and close the scissors steadily, but keep them in essentially the same position.

If the design is large, divided it into workable sections of about eight inches. If you separate the design at connecting points the pieces will still glue together without revealing the break.

Start by trimming away excess paper around the design. Next, cut away interior spaces, and, lastly, follow the contours of the shape. If parts are very fine and have appendages, such as stems, cut bridges that attach the thin section to the body of the design. These can be cut away later. Take license with your scissors. Eliminate areas that do not fit and are not relevant to the design.

Before or after cutting, prepare the surface of the object by treating it the traditional way. Wood should be sealed, unless acrylic paint is used to color it. Metal should be free of peeling finishes and rust; paint metal surfaces with a rust preventative. Ceramic, glass, and acrylic should be clean and free of grease.

Before gluing, tack the design into place with Plasti-Tak for a dry run. Plasti-Tak will peel away easily, and it will not mar the surface. If you use Elmer's glue, sobo, or Duratite, thin the glue somewhat with water. Heavier papers will require thicker glues than thinner papers. Any precise gluing that requires extended manipulation of the design should be planned for by adding a very small amount of glycerine to the glue. This will extend the working time by making the glue dry more slowly.

Mix the glue in a small ceramic or glass container. Have a small sponge on hand. Glue should be applied sparingly and *no* air bubbles should remain under your design. Air bubbles can ruin the work by popping up later in an unsightly way. Too much glue will cause the paper to wrinkle.

Apply glue to the surface of the object, not the paper. (Only when attaching foil papers is glue applied to the paper.) Use your finger or a brush to distribute the glue evenly. Attach the design and press away air and excess glue with a water-moist sponge; start from the center of the paper and keep working out to the edges. Keep pressing lightly until the entire piece is attached and no edges stick up. Follow the contours along stems and inner and outer edges. Keep your fingers rinsed. Do not let them get tacky, because they will stick to the paper and pull it away. Once the glue dries you cannot easily remove the design; do not try.

When the glue is set and dry, you are ready to varnish. Get a clear, transparent, colorless varnish. There are many on the market compounded specifically for decoupage. Paint stores also sell varnishes for furniture and floor finishes. Read the label, and be certain that it will not discolor. Do not try to store varnish for a long period of time. Buy small cans instead.

Varnishing is a long-range process. It requires many coats—up to twenty or thirty—a clean, dry room, a clean brush, and elbow grease.

Use a chiseled oxhair varnish brush if possible. Buy the best quality so that it will not shed hair. Tackcloth is useful for removing dust and dirt before each coat.

Do not mix coatings or brushes. Keep turpentine soluble varnish brushes together, lacquer thinner brushes together, water soluble brushes together, and keep them all *apart!*

Apply varnish according to the instructions on the varnish can label. Follow these instructions meticulously. Each varnish requires different treatment. Pay particular attention to whether the varnish needs to be stirred before using, how long it takes to dry before the next application is made, and any specifics about techniques of application. Some varnishes need to be flowed on; others require skimpy coatings.

Usually start varnishing from the middle of the surface; work toward the outer edges with arclike strokes. Take care to avoid excessive air bubbles. Brush with the grain of the wood for your first coat. Successive strokes should be brushed in the opposite direction.

If a gloss varnish is used for the varnish building process it is often more attractive to complete varnishing with two coats of matte varnish.

After five or six coats of varnish are dry and hard, sand with a mixture of soap flakes and water using #400 wet-or-dry sandpaper. Soap flakes act as an emulsion. You can also dry-sand. When the surface is smooth, rinse with cold water and dry. Dust it with tackcloth and build more coats of varnish. Allow the recommended drying time between each coat. Continue varnishing, and periodically sand until the decoration is buried in varnish.

To eliminate faint scratches for a final finish, rub the surface with a slight paste of rottenstone or pumice powder mixed with lemon or linseed oil. Apply it in a circular motion with a pad of flannel or nylon stocking. The object should have a superb finish. Apply a clear wax such as Butcher's Wax on a dampened piece of flannel. Allow the wax to dry, and buff the surface with another clean, damp piece of cotton flannel.

Always varnish the inside or underside of your objects with a few coats, even if you are going to line the form.

A hint: when varnishing make certain that excess varnish does not drip to the underside down the sides of the piece. It makes it difficult to sand later. Wipe drips away with a lint-free cloth.

Specific techniques that take license with the traditional decoupage process described above are detailed in the captions of these illustrations.

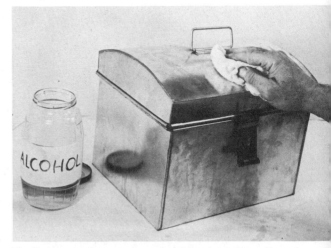

The first step in decoupaging a metal box is to clean off the protective oils with alcohol.

Next, paint all parts with a rust-preventive paint.

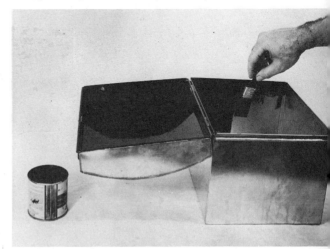

The design is layed out on a Japanese textured paper using an explosion design. (See Chapter 3.)

Then it is cut out and "exploded" by separating elements.

The central stem of the design is custom fitted.

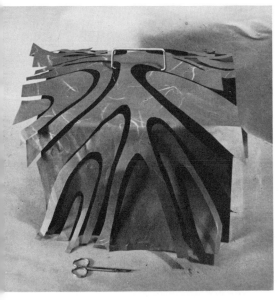

Using Plasti-Tak, the parts are temporarily attached to fit parts into place on the front . . .

. . . and on the back. After the temporary putty adhesive is removed, the design is glued in place with diluted white glue. When the glue has dried, 17 coats are applied to the box.

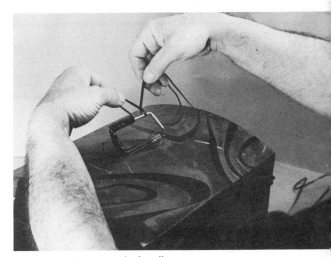

Lacing is used to cover the handle.

In some cases the form of an object is so important that it should not be detracted from with decorations. In this case, however, the design transports this tin deed box from an ordinary to a handsome container. From *Contemporary Decoupage* by Thelma R. Newman

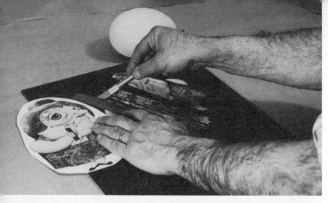

One of the challenges in paper art is to fit a flat piece of paper onto a curved surface. The technique is called "fragmentation." Very thin strips of a picture are cut.

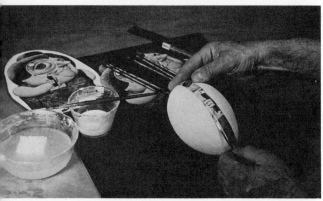

Over an expanded polystyrene egg that had been coated with three coats of acrylic gesso, parts of the picture were glued down, strip by strip, not allowing any background to show. Some very fine wedges of picture are eliminated so that the picture fits over the curved areas.

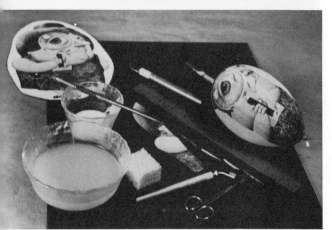

Some areas are cut into contours following the curves of the design. For this kind of cutting, a swivel cutter was used, the same employed in cutting the paper mola (Chapter 3).

Many coats of varnish are applied, one day for each coat, until 15 coats are applied. The whole is sanded and waxed.

Imperiously, our lady looks through her magnifying glass monocle. She is somewhat reduced from her original bulk, but remains very much the same person. Fragmentation is one way for a body to lose some weight. Courtesy: American Crayon Co., From Contemporary Decoupage

Carl Federer's fragmented design on a real egg.

A decoupaged tissue box using metal-coated paper and trim.

Elements of a collograph print by Fran Willner were used to decoupage this wood box.

This lamp is decoupaged with cutout elements of gift wrap on the inside of an acrylic cylinder. Open spaces were finished with a metallic paint. The crystallike ornament is a polyhedron of acrylic decoupaged on five facets with watercolored Japanese lattice textured paper. The chest (bookcase) is done in the *trompe l'oeil* style. It is a tongue-in-cheek technique that simulates reality by painting in shadows and depth lines following the rules of perspective. Parts of book jackets were cut, arranged, glued, and painted to look like the real thing. Then the whole is varnished and sanded as in traditional decoupage. From *Contemporary Decoupage* by Thelma R. Newman

181

This hutch chair-table was designed by Jane Bearman (inside) and Thelma R. Newman (top). Glazed colored papers were used with metallized paper trims. A urethane varnish was utilized to embed the paper elements.

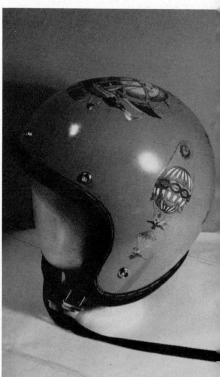

Almost any object can be decoupaged. Dee Davies and Dee Frankel created this headgear.

Any material can be decoupaged. This is a stoneware bowl decoupaged with elements from a gift wrap and then varnished with a urethane spray.

A screen of corrugated cardboard (from a Dritz cutting board for sewing) was papered with metal coated paper and then decorated with flowers cut from a *Foster Art Print Book* of Oriental flowers and varnished with Mod-Podge, a polyvinyl acetate-type of coating. Courtesy: Foster Art Books

Papier-Mâché

Papier-mâché, made of common materials —paper and glue—has been used for centuries to make festival objects, usually with religious symbolism. It has also been both covering and structure for furniture, bowls, other containers, lampshades, and a variety of decorative objects. In all corners of the world—Russia, India, Mexico, and Japan—

papier-mâché has been brought to a fine art. Relatively recently papier-mâché has been used for stage sets and props and for window display figures.

Because papier-mâché is a very strong material, particularly with the application of new plastic glues and finishes, it has also been employed in sculptures where one expects relative permanence.

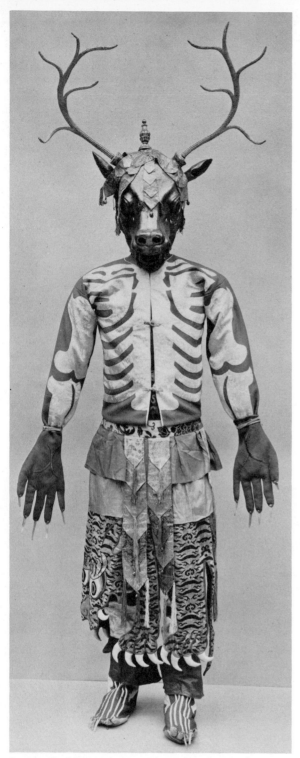

Lamaist devil-dance costume with an animal mask of papier-mâché. From Tibet, early 19th century. Courtesy: Metropolitan Museum of Art

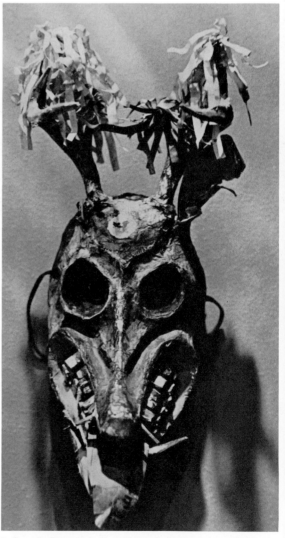

A Cora Indian mask from Nayarit, Mexico, is used to celebrate Easter and is made of papier-mâché.

A traditional "Thai" gold-leafed and lacquered papier-mâché owl-shaped box. These are made in Thailand and in larger quantities in Burma.

Another Cora Indian mask.

The practice of making masks of papier-mâché is almost universal. This mask comes from El Salvador.

Papier-mâché has been used traditionally in Asia and more recently in the West for stage props and masks. In this photo Apollo protects Orestes from the charge of matricide. Courtesy: Guthrie Theater Co., Minneapolis/St. Paul

Here in papier-mâché Clytemnestra welcomes her husband Agamemnon. Courtesy: Guthrie Theater Co., Minneapolis/St. Paul

PAPIER-MÂCHÉ PROCESSES

Papier-mâché knows no limits as to what it can become as an object. There are four basic techniques that cover all possibilities. Papier-mâché can be applied over existing objects as a finish or refurbish. It can be made into a mash, and forms can be constructed from the mash almost like hand-building of pottery; papier-mâché also can be applied over some kind of an armature or skeletal structure, or it can be formed in a mold. Each process is capable of supporting numerous variations of the basic concepts. What is important to note is that papier-mâché is a plastic medium and can easily express almost any craft or fine art idea.

The papier-mâché product now has a potential for permanence whereas, once, when wheat paste and fish glues were used, the paper, if not properly coated, decomposed in time.

APPLYING PAPIER-MÂCHÉ OVER AN OBJECT

This is a very simple technique. Start with an object—as temporary as a cardboard box or milk carton, or as long-lasting as a piece of furniture. Select the type of paper you wish to use as a covering—newspaper, paper toweling, *kozo*, or any paper that is absorbent enough to allow the adhesive to penetrate its fibers.

The adhesive should be one of the plastics—from the powdered vinyl called Metylan which needs to be mixed with water, or polyvinyl acetate types such as Elmer's glue, Sobo, Duratite, Wil-hold, and so on. These are milky-white, water-soluble glues that dry to a clear substance that becomes water resistant. If you have worked with papier-mâché before

and have used wheat paste (wallpaper paste), give it up. The new wallpaper pastes made of vinyl are far superior.

Now, with paper and adhesive on hand, all you need are containers to hold the glue and water—the p.v.a. (polyvinyl acetate) glues should be mixed 3 parts glue to 1 part water—scissors (optional), and your object. If you are covering furniture, sand the surface to clean off dirt and to give it "tooth."

Tearing paper allows edges to disappear, one layer fitting into another when the paper has been soaked in glue and laid on the surface of the object. But if you want patterns, do not tear, but cut your pieces into shapes like triangles, squares, or circles, to name three successful design possibilities. Overlap the shapes in a formal pattern like fish scales, or in a random arrangement.

The number of layers depends on the function and what you are making. A thicker application of about four layers yields a stronger surface than just one layer. Papier-mâché can be patched, filled, and repaired easily.

Finishing comes after the paper has dried. The surface can be sanded smooth, if desired, and should be sealed in any case. Take care to use compatible materials in your sealers, base coats, and finishes—some repel one another, resulting in separation. Read the labels on cans carefully. If you are in doubt, make a test on scrap material. A sealer and base coat that works well is acrylic modeling paste, diluted with water to a brushable consistency, or acrylic emulsion (sometimes referred to as polymer emulsion). Even more glue (p.v.a.) brushed over the surface will seal the paper and keep it from absorbing too much paint. The paint base coat can also be acrylic paint and the final finish can be acrylic emulsion as well. Mod Podge, which is a polyvinyl acetate, provides a good finish. For a very hard surface use a plastic varnish such as polyurethane or vinyl. Certainly, if you are covering a piece of furniture you will want to use a more durable finish. Acrylic is longer lasting and tougher than polyvinyl acetate, and polyurethane is the toughest.

Any form can be used as a mold if it does not have under-cuts. Protect the mold with a coating of green soap, petroleum jelly, or, as in this case, a piece of Mylar wrap. Cut pieces of paper; dip them in a diluted solution of p.v.a., and apply the paper around the mold, overlapping. Add as many layers as necessary to achieve the thickness you need.

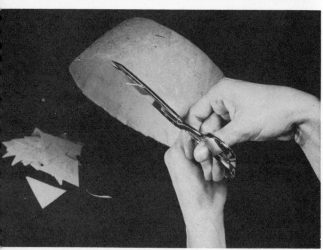

Allow the form to dry on the mold. Then remove it and trim the edge.

With more of the same paper, finish the edge by wrapping glue-saturated paper around it. We also lined the bowl with pieces of the same decorative Japanese paper.

The triangular "hard edge" line of paper units is utilized to create a pattern in this paper bowl.

PAPIER-MÂCHÉ AS A MASH

Mash or paper pulp can be made or purchased prepared for use. To make a mash, tear four sheets of newspaper, or a similar quantity of tissues or paper toweling, into small pieces about one inch square. Place them in a pan with enough hot water to cover, and soak for several hours. If you have a blender, beat the mash to a pulp working with plenty of water and with small batches. It takes only seconds to mash. If you do not have a blender, place the paper in a strainer and mash the paper until all the water is removed.

Then to the mash add 2 tablespoons of whiting, 4 tablespoons of polyvinyl acetate (white glue) as a binder, and stir until the pulp has a claylike consistency. You may want to add 1 tablespoon of linseed oil; it helps make the mash more workable and the final result a bit tougher. Also, a few drops of oil of wintergreen or oil of cloves will keep the mash from turning sour. Keeping mash in a plastic bag in the refrigerator will also extend its working life.

Prepared mixtures that only require the addition of water are sold under the trade names of Celluclay and Shreddi-Mix.

Following the directions on the package, the mix is kneaded with water until it handles like clay.

A wad is flattened on a piece of waxed paper. Two guides that act as a thickness gauge are placed on each side of the mixture.

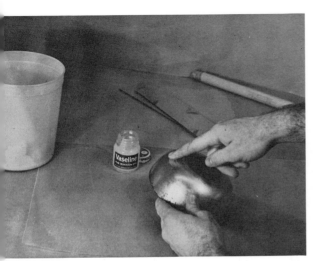

Papier-mâché mash can be used with or without a mold. In this case, a "mold" is coated with petroleum jelly.

A piece of waxed paper is placed on top and a dowel (or rolling pin) is used to roll the papier-mâché mash into a pancake. Notice that the rolling pin will rest on the two guides, thereby determining the thickness of the final piece.

A pizza cutter is used to trim away the excess.

The papier-mâché pancake is placed over the coated mold . . .

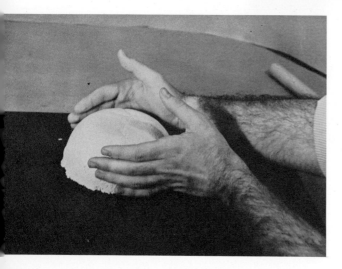

. . . and pressed to the shape of the mold.

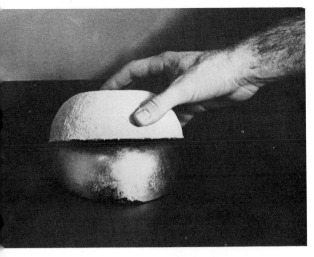

When dry, the piece is removed.

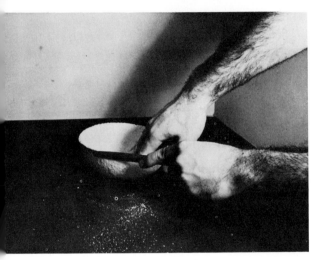

Edges and rough areas are filed and sanded.

Alcohol is used to wipe away petroleum jelly that was transferred to the form.

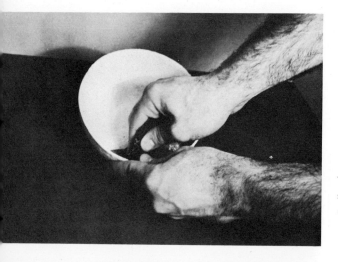

The interior is sanded to a smoother finish than the outside, which is allowed to retain the characteristic roughness of papier-mâché mash.

Both interior and exterior are coated with three layers of acrylic gesso.

A paper form is cut for decoupaging the interior of the bowl.

Parts are cut away and reorganized to fit the bowl . . .

. . . and tacked in place temporarily with Plasti-Tak. Then the pieces are glued to the bowl with diluted polyvinyl acetate (white glue).

Connections and white edges are touched up with black acrylic paint to match the outlines.

A two-part mixture of water and clear white epoxy is mixed and evenly applied to the interior with a spatula. In one application, the epoxy takes the place of at least 20 coats of varnish. It provides a hard, clear, ceramic effect surface.

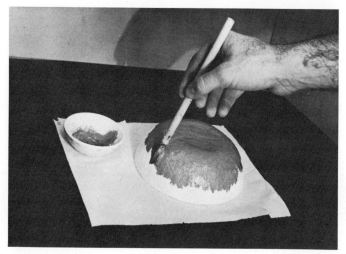

The exterior is painted with orange acrylic paint, and, when it was thoroughly dry, the surface was given five protective coats of clear varnish.

The completed bowl, which was only a hunk of mash a few days before, is now a handsome form with a marvelous washable coating. There was absolutely no warping of the form.

Papier-mâché mash—just like clay—can also be molded into novelty shapes and puppet heads.

These comic faces are painted with acrylic gesso after they have dried.

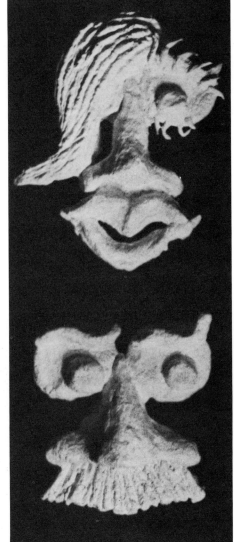

The completed comic masks are left unpainted and unglazed.

SOME TECHNIQUES

Papier-mâché mash can be squeezed, rolled, pinched, smoothed, much like clay. The result is a solid piece, unless excess is scooped out of the back or nonvisible side. Or it can be rolled out into a pancake and shaped over a mold, as detailed in the following photo sequence.

Mash makes for excellent detail on another kind of papier-mâché base. It can, if reinforced, make excellent handles, knobs, or other projections. The surface of the mash can be smoothed with a spatula, but it always retains a characteristic rough texture.

PAPIER-MÂCHÉ OVER AN ARMATURE

Papier-mâché can be formed over temporary or permanent armatures that give the final structure support. A temporary armature could be a paper or plastic bag stuffed with newspaper, or a blown up balloon. The bag can be "removed" by emptying its contents. The balloon can be removed by deflating it, leaving a hollow shell. This technique reduces the weight of the form greatly and is excellent for mask making.

Permanent armatures are made from wires of various sorts, from soft aluminum armature wire to other, stronger (nonrusting) types, or armatures can be shaped from chicken wire, carpenter's cloth, or from boxes, cans, and scrap materials of different sorts that have been attached securely.

The basic technique is detailed in the forming of "Maxima Minnie." Huge forms can be made this way.

The completed frame is balanced and padded where needed.

More padding of newspaper is taped over the frame.

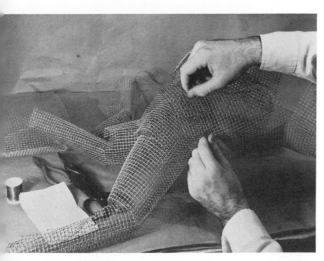

Papier-mâché is often applied over an armature or permanent base such as this carpenter cloth frame.

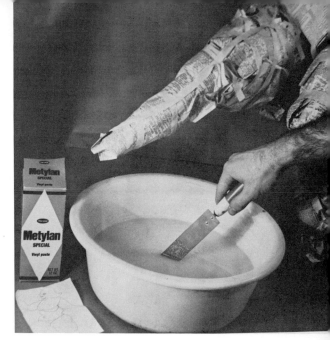

A vinyl wallpaper paste is mixed with water following the directions on the package.

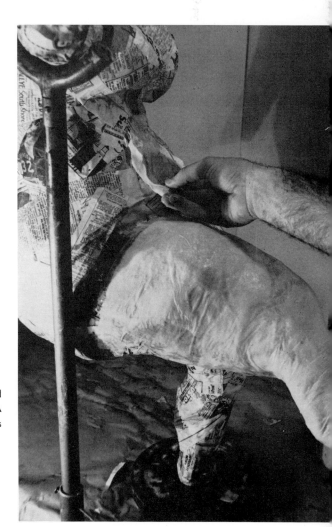

Strips of newspaper are layered over the entire form until a thickness of at least four layers has been achieved. A final layer of paper toweling is added because it accepts paint well.

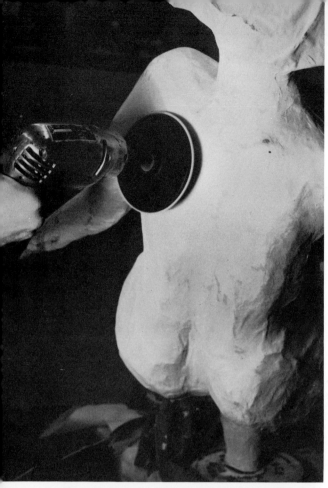

Sand and patch rough areas.

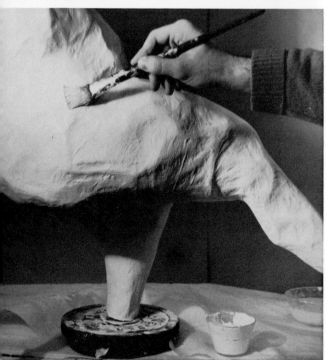

The form is painted with acrylic paint and "Maxima Minnie" is decorated, decoupage style, with a bikini, hair, hat, face, and trimmings.

A base is prepared by spraying a release coating into a polyethylene basin.

Polyester resin, catalyst, and color are mixed thoroughly.

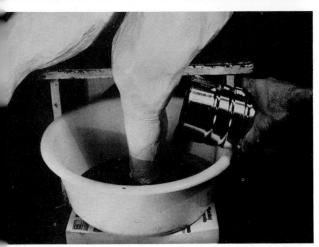

Maxima Minnie's leg is positioned in the basin and the liquid polyester resin is poured around it.

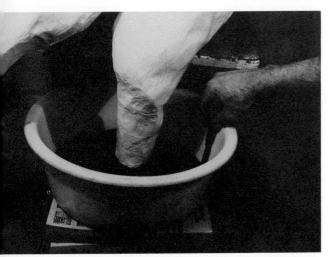

When the resin has cured it is very hard. A knife is used to loosen the base form from its mold.

Two positions of Maxima Minnie all set to take a plunge.

PAPIER-MÂCHÉ OVER OR IN A MOLD

This approach uses papier-mâché in or over some kind of mold. The paper form is removed from the mold, and, if it is in parts, these sections are glued together with more papier-mâché. With this technique you can re-create a form or use a basic shape without destroying the original.

It is essential that a separating or release material be used to keep the paper binder or adhesive from sticking to the mold. A light coating of talc, vaseline, aluminum foil, or plastic wraps such as Saran makes separation easy. Molds may be made of wood, metal, ceramic, plaster, silicone rubber—in fact, almost anything. If the mold has under-cuts (projections that would lock the paper in place when dry), then the papier-mâché has to be applied in sections and then taped together after the pieces have dried.

Use either paper mash or torn paper strips to line the mold. Allow the paper to stay in place until thoroughly dry; this minimizes warpage.

A superstition figure of a skeleton-siren from Mexico is made over a wadding of newspaper.

Festival figures such as this one from Mexico are made around a coil of paper so that fire-crackers can be inserted to blow them up.

A Jeanne Valentine cat is production-made in a mold and is masterfully hand-finished, painted, and glazed. Courtesy: Fred Leighton's

A basket of beautifully formed papier-mâché vegetables with realistic details, from Mexico.

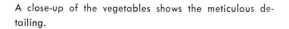

A close-up of the vegetables shows the meticulous detailing.

Fantasy-religious figures formed in wire are covered with papier-mâché. The figure on the left is by Saulo Moreno of Mexico City. The skeleton is used to celebrate All Souls' Day.

Piñatas are an old tradition in Spain, Mexico, and Central and South America. The central form is made of hollow, heavy paper which is covered with papier-mâché and decorated with tissue paper or crepe paper fringing. These are large forms that are filled with goodies for children. Piñatas are broken open at party time by blindfolded children wielding sticks. Courtesy: Fred Leighton's

Two Christmastime primitive toys in papier-mâché from Mexico. They are hollow.

Colored papers have been dipped in paste and modeled over a base. Different papers impart the various textures.

Another view of the lady from Mexico. Brushing the form with acrylic paint and then rubbing some off creates the antiqued effect. The whole is glazed with acrylic emulsion.

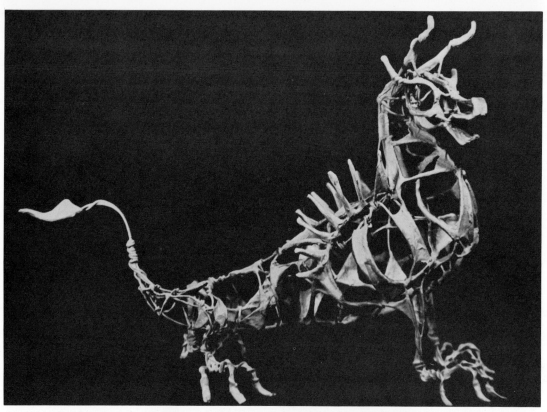

A dragon of papier-mâché over a wire frame by Saulo Moreno. Parts are filled by a thin web of paper.

Papier-mâché over wood frames a mirror (on the reverse side). Leaves are detailed with glue-coated string. Petals are shaped of paper saturated with glue.

Kashmiri pillboxes lacquered and decorated over papier-mâché. Courtesy: Brimful House

Kashmiri pins of papier-mâché. They are lightweight yet sturdy. Courtesy: Brimful House

Kashmiri papier-mâché bracelets are finely finished. Courtesy: Brimful House

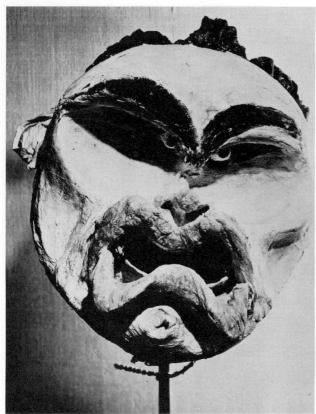

Papier-mâché sculpture, life-size, of "Wallace," by Gerald Scarfe.
Courtesy: Waddell Gallery

"Humphrey" in papier-mâché by Gerald Scarfe. Courtesy: Wadde
Gallery

Gerald Scarfe, "Nixon," life-size papier-mâché. Courtesy: Waddell Gallery

Each personality is fully developed. This is "Pirate Jean LeFarge."

A close-up showing details of Pirate LeFarge's face and elegantly painted eyes and mustache.

More sophisticated are these marionettes by Marjorie Moore. They are papier-mâché characters with an identity. These are "Emily Engle and Jordie Jester."

Marjorie Moore's friend "Gloria Grownup" . . .

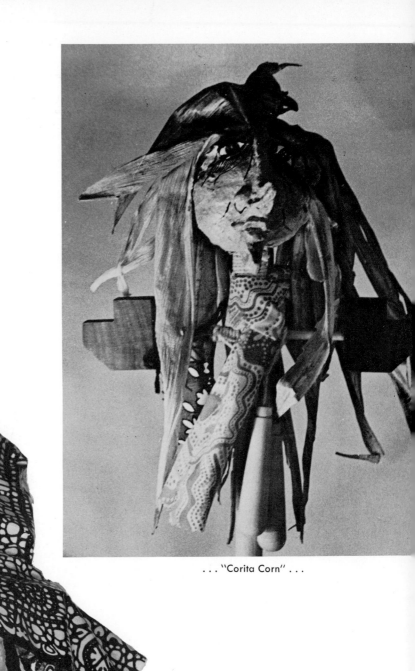

. . . "Corita Corn" . . .

. . . and "Sylvia Scarecrow" also by Marjorie Moore.

chapter 8

Decorative Papers and Bookbinding

Decorative Papers

Decorative papers have existed almost as long as paper. Surfaces were decorated for their own sake or as a design experiment for textiles. In fact, almost any textile decorating technique is applicable to paper. There are so many that only a few concepts are covered here.

Some of the ways papers can be decorated are by stamping and printing, using resist materials such as paste or wax (batik), stencil, fold and dye, tye and dye, silk-screening, marbling, painting—watercolor, acrylic, starch paint.

STAMPING AND PRINTING

Designs for printing can be cut from many materials: vegetables, such as pota-

toes, wood, Styrofoam, urethane foam, linoleum, vinyl, cardboard, rubber from tires, erasers, or RTV silicone, scrap objects like screws, spools, sponges, leaves, washers, and so on. In fact, whatever can be cut into or whatever has a ready-made pattern can be utilized. These objects can be inked and used as stamping patterns. Tempera paint can be applied to the printing surface with a brush. Printing or block printing ink can be applied to a sponge that can be used as a stamp pad, or color can be rolled on from an inking tray via a brayer.

Designs can be repeated in several ways. Some methods for joining one unit to another are: with a random effect, where your eye judges negative and positive space relationships and the distribution of texture and color; repeat designs that line up blocks

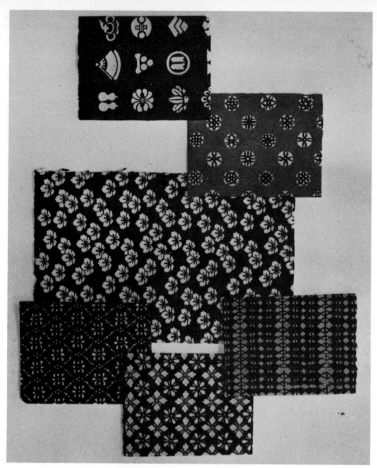

An assortment of decorative papers made by stamping and printing with small units. Courtesy: Florence Temko

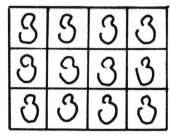

Block Repeat

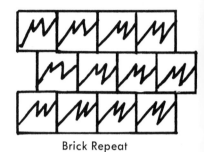

Brick Repeat

Half –Drop Repeat

one over the other, like bricks in a wall, half dropped blocks in alternating columns; angle repeats such as diamond shapes and the repeat design. Butt joints allow units to meet in straight lines. Dovetail joints permit one unit to fit into another without overlapping. And overlapping joints occur where units overlap.

A Japanese paper in one color using a block repeat.

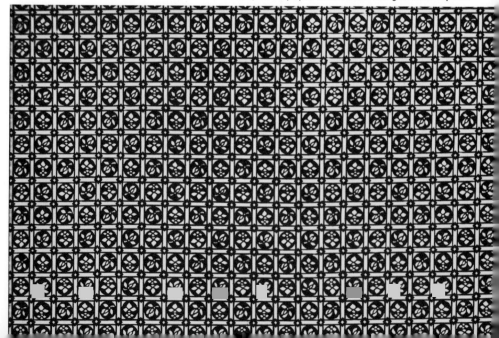

Diagonal Repeat

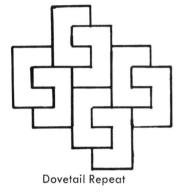

Dovetail Repeat

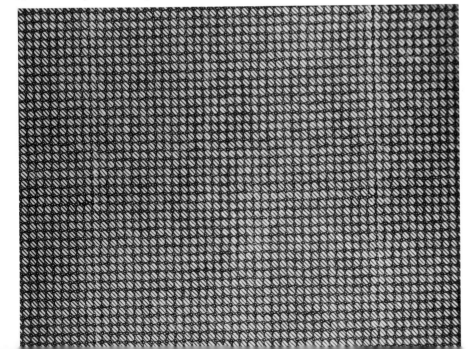

Another Japanese repeat with different color circles superimposed over alternating design units.

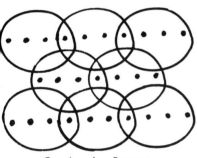

Overlapping Repeat

Ways of repeating designs include units that butt against one another in straight lines such as the block repeat, the brick repeat with its horizontal emphasis, the half-drop repeat with a vertical emphasis, and angle repeats using diagonals. Dovetail repeats allow one unit to fit into another, and overlapping superimposes one part of a unit over another.

A two-color Japanese hand-printed design.

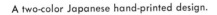

215

STARCH PAPERS

Starch papers were used by early bookbinders for covering books. It is a technique that is very similar in effect to fingerpainting without using fingers. To make starch paint mix two tablespoons of cornstarch with two tablespoons of cold water in a pot. Add one cup of boiling water and bring the whole to a boil while stirring constantly. When the mixture is cool it becomes the binder for color. Add powdered batik dyes or acrylic paint to the base for color. Store it in jars. A drop of oil of cloves will help to preserve the color. You can also use prepared finger paint.

Brush the wet colored mixture, as evenly as possible, on the paper, and press a hard object into the paint. The printing block can be a potato, a cardboard comb, a linoleum block or woodcut, etc. If there is a mistake, more paint can be brushed on and the block printed again. You can also press a piece of cardboard or another piece of paper on top, draw a pattern or apply pressure with your fingers and then quickly pull away the cardboard or paper to reveal a textured, blotted design.

Combed paper patterns can be made by pulling a cardboard comb through the wet starch paint. Pressure will scrape away lines of paint, revealing the paper.

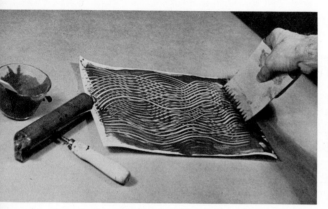

A cooked starch mixture is brushed over paper and a design is scraped into the color with a cardboard.

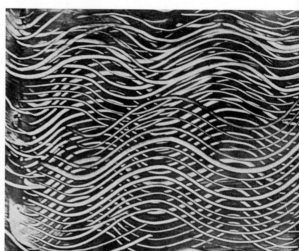

The completed design dries into a semigloss finish. Raised areas that were apparent when the starch was wet dry flat.

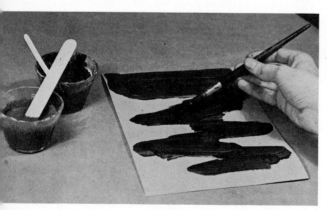

Another decorative technique using starch colors uses patterns of starch color that is brushed on a paper or cardboard "plate."

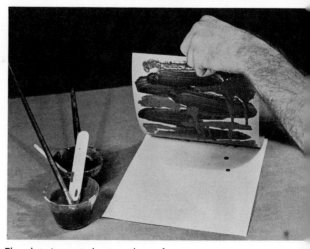

The plate is pressed onto a sheet of paper.

A decorative effect results.

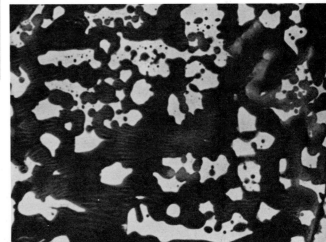

Another example of starch printing.

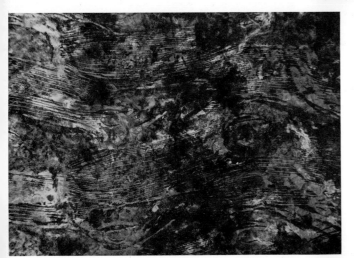

Starch combing is superimposed over a random paint effect on a metallic paper. The resulting texture is very rich.

Starch paint using the printing "plate" concept.

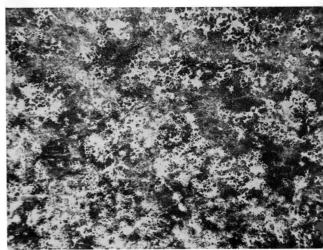

STENCILS

Stencils are cut from oaktag or a heavily waxed paper. Negative spaces are cut with a stencil knife into the paper. Then, with a stencil brush in a daubing motion, up and down, color is stippled into the cut patterns.

Stencils have thin bridges of paper from one area to another because connectors are necessary to hold one part of the design to another.

This 19th century paper stencil (9⅞″ × 16″) from Japan was used to decorate either paper or fabric. Note how fine lines are connected by bridges to heavier areas. Courtesy: The Metropolitan Museum of Art, Gift of Leon Dabo

This paper stencil was specifically made to decorate textiles, hence its larger size (31″ × 17¾″). It is Japanese and dates back to the Takugawa Period (1615–1867). Each line connects to another line, and each space is a self-contained area completely surrounded by line (paper). Courtesy: The Metropolitan Museum of Art, Gift of Clarence McK. Lewis

FOLD AND DYE

One of the most dramatic and successful techniques for decorating paper utilizes a soft absorbent paper such as the Japanese papers of the *hoshoshi* type: *gasenchi, echizen,* mulberry student grade, *torinokogami,* or *minogami.* Paper toweling can also be used, or linoleum block printing papers. Colorants can be watercolor, food dye, batik dye, or India ink. They are all water soluble.

There are several basic ways to fold paper for dyeing. Each begins by folding the paper into accordion pleats along the length of the paper. This makes for a repeat design along one axis.

One variation is to fold the accordion pleated strip to produce square or rectangular areas—effectively pleating the paper along a perpendicular axis. Another folding design is to fold the paper accordion fashion into a series of equilaterial (60°) or isosceles (45°, 90°, 45°) triangles.

For repeat designs, folds should all be the same size. The thinner the paper the more folds possible.

Uneven and irregular folding is another variation. Instead of folding the sheet into an accordion with equal pleats, try unequal widths. Or fold the paper into a fan shape and then into triangles, or random shapes. Each fold will produce a very different effect.

The next step is to dip the folded paper into dyes. The area, colors, and position of the dyeing will determine the shapes and colors in the repeat design. Try dipping just corners, then edges. Dip into one color first, then a second, and even a third. Permit different degrees of color saturation by removing the paper more quickly or allowing the paper to absorb more color—thereby dyeing a larger area. The amount of pressure you apply with your fingers (or with a pliers) will help distribute the color. Designs vary according to the amount of pressure applied. After the dyeing process, very gently open the wet paper and place it on newspaper to dry. When dry, you can press it with a warm iron to press out the folds; always press through several sheets of newspaper.

Fold a soft paper into accordion pleats.

Then fold the accordion pleats into equilateral triangles which also form pleats.

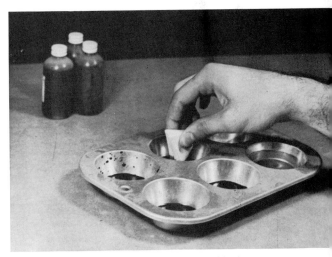

Dip corners into different colors of water soluble dyes.

Continue the process, sometimes overlapping colors.

Very carefully open the wet paper.

Place the paper flat on newspaper to dry.

The finished piece is pressed between newspaper with a warm iron.

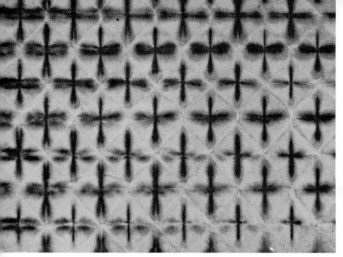

Another example of fold and dye.

An example of fold and dye, folded the same way, can be different depending on whether colors are overlapped, how long they are left in the dye, and how hard the paper is pressed with the fingers to encourage the dye to spread.

One section of a fold and dye using equilateral triangles.

A square folded dyed paper.

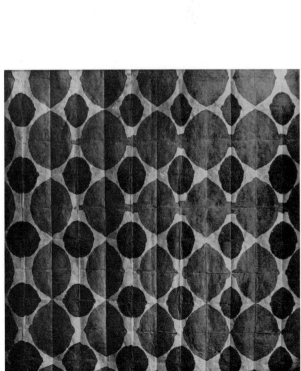

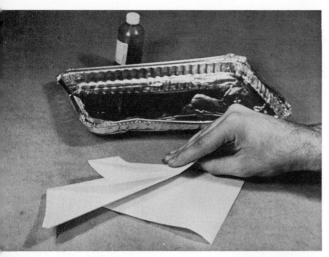

Folding can take many forms, such as this diagonal.

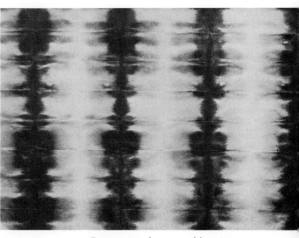

Even rectangles can add variety.

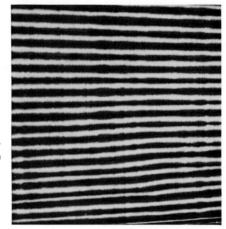

Or a straight folded accordion sheet, dipped into a light color and then into a dark color.

TIE AND DYE

Tie and dye or tie-dyeing is a resist-dyeing process that consists of knotting, binding, folding, or sewing paper in various ways so that when it is dyed the dye cannot penetrate the tied areas.

Tie-dye also dates back to the Orient in practice. The Japanese make a beautiful decorative paper using spot techniques called *shibori*. In China, the craft, using spot sewing and folding, is known as *tritik*, in Malay *plangi*, and in West Nigeria *adire*, *adire ido*, or *adire alabere*. Indigo was the usual dye coloring. Indians used a *tritik* technique in Mexico, Central America, and South America as well.

To tie-dye, use the same soft paper as in paper fold and dye. Prepare the paper by folding, knotting, binding, sewing, or a combination of these. Coat the string with wax or use rubber bands to effect certain bindings. These prevent dye from being absorbed under and through the string and maintain the original color of the paper.

Tying can be accomplished three basic ways. A length of paper can be folded or gathered and tied at intervals. A square or rectangle can be folded from the center out and tied, or knots can be sewed or tied tightly in spots. Individual ties can be dipped in dye.

Use the same dyes as for folding and dying paper. You may dip the individual knotted areas into dye, or, starting with a light color, dip into one color first and then a second color. This creates a pattern in the dye. Knots may be held in a cluster and the background dipped into another color. Dipping an area into water first dilutes the color and softens edges, if this is what you want.

Linen threads are excellent for binding, but yarn, cord, raffia, tape, and rubber bands are good too. Use a strong thread that will permit pulling and tension. To maintain an area in a stronger pattern than waxed string

can provide, melt some paraffin and paint it around the tied string. Bindings should be taut and firm.

After dyeing to the proper degree of color intensity (colors always dry lighter), carefully untie the string and unfold the paper gently. Dry the paper on newspaper. Later, place the paper between several sheets of newspaper and press with a warm iron to remove wrinkles. It is also possible to allow the paper to dry and then untie it and press.

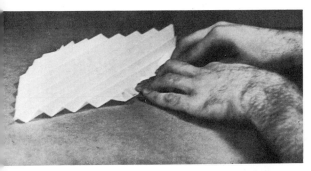

A sheet of soft paper is folded into accordion pleats.

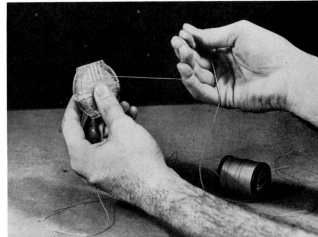

Heavy thread is waxed by running it through beeswax.

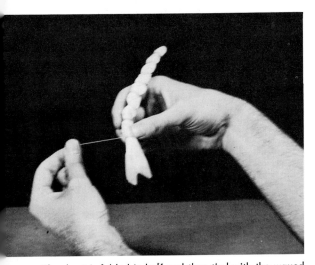

The sheet is folded in half and then tied with the waxed thread at intervals.

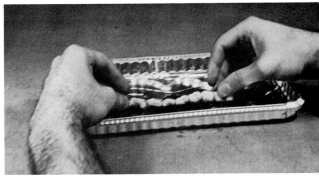

The piece is dipped into water-soluble dye of one color.

Then another section is dipped into a second color.

Remove the string carefully and unfold the wet paper.

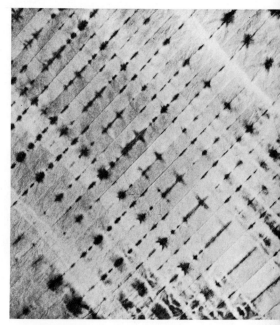

The finished tie and dye is pressed between sheets of newspaper with a warm iron to eliminate wrinkles.

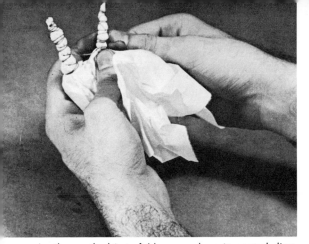

Another method is to fold paper along its central diagonal.

Each tied section is dipped into dye.

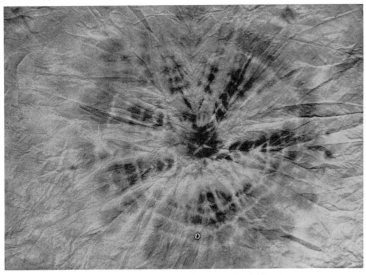

When the paper is opened it might look like this.

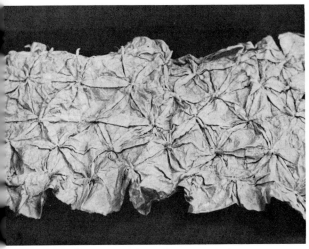

Smaller units can be tied in a repeat design.

After dyeing the entire paper it could look like this.

MARBLING

The invention of marbling was credited to the Persians about A.D. 1550. Persian marbled papers were introduced into Europe in A.D. 1590. The first examples were of the "fine combed" variety. In 1750 marbled papers were used for the first time in North American bookbindings.

Marbling produces patterns on paper that are similar in appearance to marble. Oil color is suspended on a sizing of water and carrageen moss extract or gum of tragacanth. Patterns are made in the color and the paper is placed over the pattern to lift off the color. There are many variations of this concept; all meet with varying degrees of success and different qualities of patterns.

The size, which is a gelatinous material, can vary. Carrageen moss, or Irish seaweed, is a form of algae that is found along rocky coastlines. The size is prepared by boiling a cup of carrageen moss in two quarts of soft water for about five minutes. Then add two cups of cold water and allow the mixture to stand uncovered at room temperature for 24 hours. Put it in a blender to stir away large particles, or strain it. It will last for three or four days without a preservative and can also be frozen.

Gum of tragacanth can also be used as a size. Mix ½ cup of gum of tragacanth flakes with 2 quarts of water. Allow it to sit for 24 hours. Then blend it in a blender, or strain out the lumps. The consistency should be like pourable honey.

Another size is diluted white library-type paste; add water until it pours and use that to suspend color.

Color should be oil-based: oil paint, oil-based printer's ink, etching ink. It is best to dilute these colors with mineral spirit, which works better than turpentine. The consistency should be pourable—so that you can flick the color off a straw, swab stick, brush, or nail. Any kind and color of nonglossy paper can be used.

Pour the size into a shallow tray or pan. Do not let a skin form on the size. To release surface tension, place a piece of newspaper over the size and lift it off. The consistency should permit a drop of paint to spread immediately into a large circle. If it does not, add more water. Drop different colors onto the size. Patterns can be formed with a pin comb, a nail, or thin sticks by drawing them through the color in heart shapes, repeat designs, or random patterns.

Place the paper onto the size by holding it at one end and gradually allowing it to fall onto the surface, or, by holding it up at two opposite corners, allow a diagonal sag to touch the size and then allow the corners to drop gradually onto the size. These methods help to eliminate large air bubbles which would interfere with the design.

The pattern on the size will immediately transfer to the paper. Lift off the paper and rinse away the size, or blot it off with a sponge. Set the paper on newspaper to dry, pattern upward.

Before a second pattern is made, pick up remaining ink by dropping a sheet of newspaper on the size the same way you did for transferring the original design.

If you add a few drops of ox gall to diluted oil paints you will find more life and action in the colors.

Another method of creating marbling effects is by using water in the pan instead of a size, and using colored inks instead of oil paints. Inks can be placed on the water surface with a brush charged with color. One color touched on another makes a spot within a spot without mixing. Color is less controlled on water than on a size, but some organization of color and pattern is possible. The paper is laid on the water in the same manner as in the other processes. It should be removed and allowed to dry face up on newspaper. Any surplus color on the water can be blotted off with newspaper.

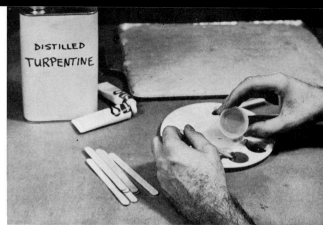

Enough water is added so that the flakes dissolve, and the mixture is blended or strained to eliminate lumps. The mixture is then poured into a shallow tray. Oil-based colors mixed with mineral spirits or turpentine are flicked off of a brush or a stick onto the size. The colors should flow.

Gum tragacanth flake is mixed with water and allowed to stand overnight.

These colors are a bit too thick, as is the gum tragacanth. Both have to be thinned, but they are still usable in the meantime.

With a swab stick (or nail) move the paint into patterns.

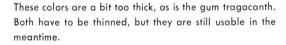

Place the paper carefully over the ink—be certain not to trap any air bubbles in the process.

A pin comb can be made to distribute color, too. Banker's pins are attached to adhesive tape which in turn is sandwiched between cardboard.

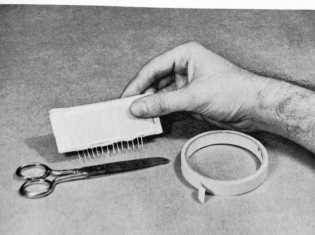

The completed design is waxed.

One marbling design. These can vary tremendously, depending on the mixture of paint, the suspension vehicle (size)—whether it is carrageen moss, gum tragacanth, or water.

Notice that a repeat pattern exists within a random design on this hand-marbled paper from England.

This pattern is even more free.

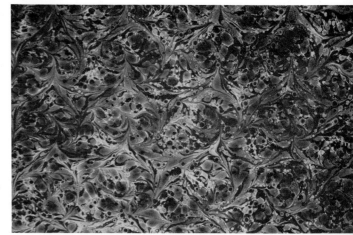

An assortment of marbled paper designs on various tints and kinds of paper.

BATIK

Batik is an old technique used for decorating fabric. It achieved excellence in Java, Indonesia. Batik is a resist technique using wax to protect areas of color, and it is applicable to paper decoration.

To make a batiked design, melt paraffin safely in an electric frying pan, a double boiler, or a crayon melter. Wax can be applied to the paper with a brush (or *tjanting* —a miniature "watering can" shape with a fine spout that is difficult to control). Coloring should be liquid and transparent such as batik dyes, India ink, or food color. Transparent color mixes differently from opaque pigments. For instance, fuchsia and yellow make red; violet and green make blue; fuchsia and green make yellow orange. When working with batik it is best to start dyeing with light colors first and successively applying darker colors.

In batiked paper, start with a white or light colored paper. Paint with wax the area you want to remain the original paper color. Then brush your first color over the entire sheet. Allow the dye to dry. Then, with wax, draw the next design component, keeping in mind that this design will be the color you just dyed the paper. Then brush on your next dye color and, if you like, continue with waxing and dyeing. The wax maintains the last color used. When finished, sandwich the batiked paper in newspaper and press with a hot iron. The newspaper will absorb the wax, leaving the batiked color only.

Working with a brush (or *tjanting*) is a controlled approach to batik design. It is possible to create very attractive random effects with dots and splashes of wax. Later, when the whole sheet has been waxed (and just before applying the last color), pop the whole sheet into the refrigerator or freezer for a few moments, then remove it and crumple the wax before adding your final dye coating. This gives a characteristic batik effect of random fine crack lines.

For batiked paper, melt paraffin safely. A crayon melter is being used here. Brush the first pattern onto the paper. Since the paper is white, these lines will be white in the finished paper.

Brush the first, lightest color dye over the areas that you want to be this color.

Dry the dye and then paint the second pattern with wax; dye the paper as shown here and repeat the process until the design is complete.

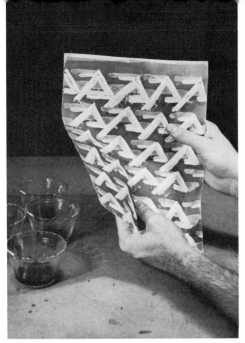

The almost finished piece is cracked to create a random dyeing effect with the last and darkest color.

The paper is placed between a sandwich of newspaper and pressed with a hot iron to melt the wax and absorb it in the newspaper.

The completed design.

Another batiked design using random splashing and dropping of wax.

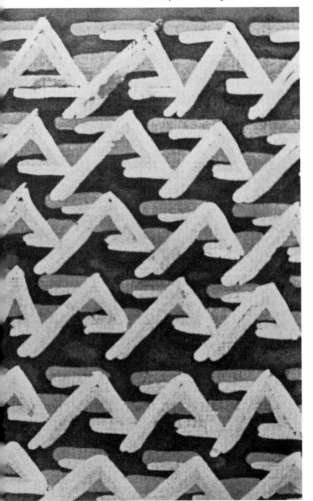

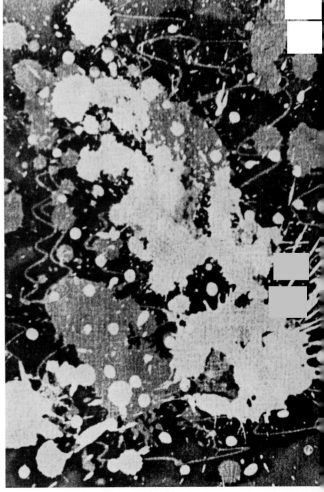

APPLICATIONS OF DECORATIVE PAPERS

Decorative papers can be used to cover various objects, small and large, from containers such as wastepaper baskets and boxes to lamps, furniture, and walls and to wrap packages. One of the oldest traditional uses for decorative paper has been to line drawers, boxes, and envelopes and to cover books, either the cover or as endpapers within the binding.

Bookbinding

Bookbinding is a paper art that is older than paper. The Chinese bound manuscripts, as did the Mayans and Aztecs. Bookbinding as we know it goes back to 200 B.C. But 3,300 years before that, the Sumerians and later the Babylonians and Assyrians produced written language on clay tablets. In transition to the bound book, writing scrolls of the Hebrews and Japanese gave way to accordion pleated parchment or vellum. Then holes were punched in margins, and the pages were tied together. Thin boards of wood were placed on the top and bottom to keep the pages flat, and eventually the pages were sewn onto bands or tapes which were then fastened to the boards. Then the books were covered with leather to conceal the tapes. Gradually, bindings became more and more elaborate. In the fourth century, bindings became very expensive and important. Some sported gold, silver, and precious jewels. It was the discovery of paper and the advent of printing, though, that catapulted the book into the forefront of communication. Today hand bookbinding is still done by a few people for those who can afford it or want books bound for special occasions. Bookbinding, though, is not difficult and can be a useful skill applicable to making diaries, photo albums, guest books, checkbook cases, address books, note pad covers, and pocketbook covers, to name a few.

Materials for bookbinding are readily available. All kinds of papers can be used for the inside—butcher, kraft, writing bond, sketching, and charcoal papers are some. The decorative covers can be made of combinations of handmade decorative papers and fabric—such as denim, hopsacking, linen, etc.—or leather. Backings of tablets and the base of book covers are chipboard, a rigid heavy cardboard. A natural-colored linen bookbinder's thread or a heavy cotton or linen thread is used for sewing signatures (groups of pages) together and to cotton twill tape that is later attached to the binder's board. Adhesives vary from rubber cement to white glues and library pastes. The glue used on the back of the book needs to be flexible such as bookbinder's glue or Sobo for leather. Cardboard for covers has to be accurately cut with square corners and straight edges. Both sides must match. Both the paper and cardboard can be cut on a paper cutter.

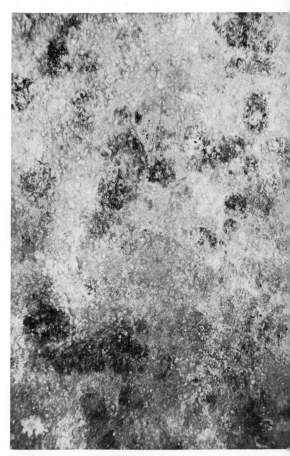

Random sponging and blotting of oil paint, superimposed from dark to light was used to create this paper.

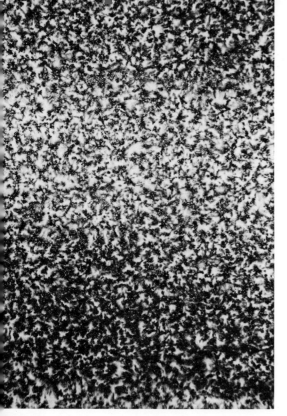

Oil color over spots of damp watercolored paper created this diffused effect. The paper was made in England.

Tools can be specialized in bookbinding like this bone folder that is used for smoothing and pressing glued areas.

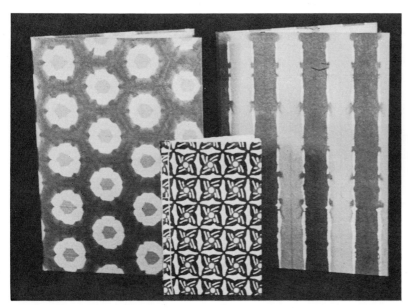

Some applications of decorative paper in portfolios and a side-sewn book, all from Japan.

TYPES OF BOOKBINDINGS

There are many styles of bookbinding. One of the earliest and simplest types is the *accordion* book. Its pages are folded back and forth like pleats and its cover is attached to the two outside sheets. This is Oriental in origin. The Chinese and Japanese still use this kind of book. Another type is the *cloth-bound* pamphlet most often used in providing permanent covers for pamphlets. The *side-sewn* book is used for binding loose single pages or pages that cannot easily be made into sections. Of all bindings, the *portfolio* is one of the simplest methods of preserving papers and is also easily made. It consists of a hard outside binding. Loose papers are placed inside. The *reverse-fold book* involves no sewing. The inside papers are folded and glued one to the other with the finished appearance like that of the side of an accordion. *Library style binding on tapes* is made by sewing folded sheets, grouped together into signatures, to tapes. The tapes, in turn, are attached to the cardboard of the covers.

There are many variations of these bookbinding styles. Sometimes methods are the same and nomenclature is different. No matter, the important thing is to be meticulous and patient when carrying out the steps in bookbinding.

THE ACCORDION BOOK

To make an accordion book take a long strip of paper and fold it back and forth to the size you want into accordion pleats. These are the pages of the book. If the paper is not long enough, glue another section to it. Place the sheets under a heavy weight to keep them flat.

Cut two pieces of chipboard 1/16 of an inch bigger on all sides than the paper. Make certain that corners are right angles. Cut the outside covering material, such as decorative paper, ¾" wider on each side than the cardboard. Put rubber cement on the board, and lay it in the center of the decorative paper. Rub it well on both sides with a clean cloth or a bone folder to make certain

all air bubbles are worked out. Cut off the corners of the decorative paper in a miter, making certain that you leave enough for the thickness of the board so that the paper can cover the edges. Apply rubber cement to the edges of the decorative paper, the part that extends all around the board. Then fold it back onto the board and press. Next, the accordion pleated paper is attached to the board. Paste each of the end sheets to the inside cover of the board. This becomes the lining sheet as well as the means for attaching the pages of the book. If you want decorative paper to be used as an end sheet, cut it to size and paste the paper over the other paper.

The accordion book, as in this Japanese version covered with tie-dye paper, is simply a long piece of paper accordion-folded and attached to a front and back cover.

CLOTH BOARD PAMPHLET

Cut a strip of cloth 2 or 3" wide and as long as the book is high, fold in the middle, and place around the back of the paper of the pamphlet. The paper is folded in half, one page fitting into the other. The pamphlet is then opened to the center and, on the fold, holes are pierced through the entire pamphlet about 2 inches apart. The sheets are sewn together this way with linen or heavy cotton thread:

tie inside

Note the direction of the thread. Dotted lines indicate the part of the thread that is inside the book.

Tie the knot on the inside of the book.

You can now attach decorative paper to the cloth backing, allowing some of the cloth to show as an edging.

A simple booklet can be made by pasting reinforcing paper on the cover (front and back pages) and sewing them together.

The sewing of these pages comes closer to regular sewing of signatures.

With reinforcing cloth vellum, the book looks like this. It is ready now for a cover and decorative paper.

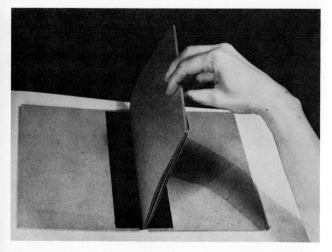

Place the bound pages over two pieces of chipboard that are $1/16''$ wider on three sides. Adhere the back cloth part to the cardboard at the inside of the book.

Cover the chipboard with decorative paper and wrap it around at least $1/2''$ on the inside.

Paste another piece of vellum over the back, concealing the sewing before pasting the decorative paper. This illustration shows the cover without decorative paper and one side with it. Complete the inside of the book by pasting a finishing piece of paper over the inside cover. If you double the finished paper and allow one side to remain unglued, it becomes a flyleaf.

PORTFOLIO

Portfolios may be designed to hold very different things—letters, sheets, charts, drawings, or stationery. The width will be determined by the rigid back part of the portfolio that is connected to a hinge of cloth or leather.

Cut two pieces of cardboard to the same size for the covers and a third piece the same length and any width for the back of the portfolio. Cut two pieces of leather, tough paper, fabric, or book vellum at least 4 inches wider than the back of the book, and 2 inches longer. This will attach the back of the portfolio to the covers and act as a hinge. Draw a line down the center of this piece to indicate the middle and glue the chipboard back piece to it. Add the cover pieces leaving about ¼ inches to ½ inches of space between the back chipboard and the side covers. Smooth out air and wrinkles. Apply glue to the top and bottom and fold it over the cardboard. Paste the other piece of leather, fabric, vellum, or paper over that area, lining the inside center of the portfolio. It should form a sandwich of covering, cardboard, and covering.

Face the covers with decorative paper as indicated in the accordion pleat book. If you want tapes or ribbons with which to tie the portfolio, now is the time to add them. Slice a parallel cut 1″ from the edge of the portfolio, string a ribbon through this and glue at least 2″ of it to the inside cover. You can now face or line the inside of the portfolio, making certain to overlap the previous pasting about ¼ inch short of the edge.

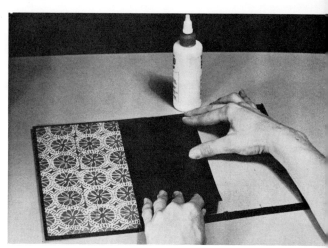

This portfolio is made of two pieces of chipboard connected by a cloth binding. The lining is made of decorative paper.

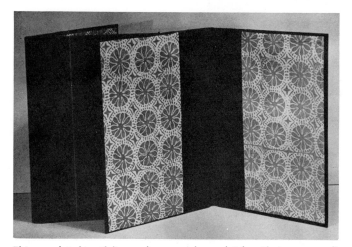

An inside piece of fabric is used as both trim and reinforcement. Decorative paper is attached last.

This completed portfolio can be covered completely with paper as well as with a cloth strip used only on the hinge area outside and inside.

The inside of a stationery portfolio from Japan.

For making a picture frame, cut four pieces of oaktag or cardboard the same size. Two of them should have openings cut out in which to frame the picture. Also cut two separate pieces of binder's cloth and one piece slightly more than double the cardboard, accommodating a hinge and the thickness of the inside frames.

Adhere the two solid pieces of cardboard to the double-sized cloth and the two frames to the single pieces. Wrap the fabric around the inside of the frame and around the outside, clipping edges so that there is no overlapping of material.

Finish the inside with decorative paper and attach the covered frames on the three outside edges, allowing the inside edge to remain unglued so that the picture can be inserted.

SIDE-SEWN BOOK

There are several methods of making a side-sewn book which actually are just different sewing patterns. Loose pages or paper folded in half can be used for this kind of book.

Cut the papers to size. Also, if you would like a soft cover, cut two pieces of decorative paper the same size as the rest of the paper. Draw a line ½" from the edge parallel to the edge. Then make a series of holes with an awl or ice pick down the line to accommodate needle and thread. The spaces between holes should be evenly divided or grouped in patterns. If the book is to be very thick, place the pages in a vise and drill fine holes with a drill. Clamp the pages together with a clothespin, spring clamp, or C clamp. Material for sewing can be cord, yarn, linen, raffia, leather tonging, or heavy cotton.

If you wish a cloth backing, add a piece of cloth and sew that on at the same time. Sewing is simply a matter of carrying the thread through each successive hole until it has passed through each hole three times (and around the back if you are to use the Japanese approach). Keep retracing steps until all the holes are filled. You should return to the beginning hole when finished, and tie end and beginning threads together.

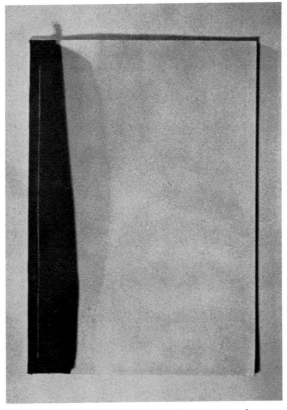

This is a side-sewn book that can bind loose pieces of paper. Note that the sewing is not on the inside but on the outside edge.

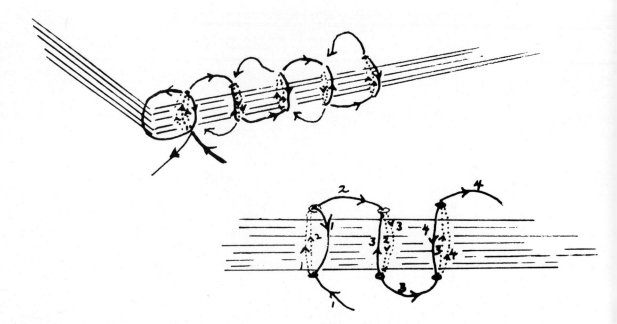

This side-sewn book is an attachment of single or double sheets of paper. It is similar to the previous side-sewn book except that instead of using cloth to back the book, thread is sewn around the back as well. Dotted lines indicate the sequence of sewing, and arrows denote the direction.

Two examples of Japanese-style side-sewn books. The book on the right has a strip of reinforcing tape on the top and bottom formed like a box to protect edges.

REVERSE-FOLD BOOK

The reverse-fold book requires no sewing. Cut the paper twice the width and fold it in half as in a booklet. Fold each pair of pages. Then fold another sheet in 1″ accordion pleats and glue each page between the Vs in the accordion sheets. Attach the accordion pleat to either a heavy cover of chipboard or a soft decorative paper. Line the board and inside cover. The last folds of the accordion should be glued to the cover and this covered with endpaper or lining.

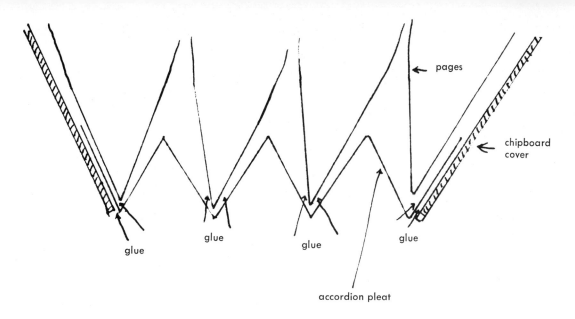

The reverse fold book is attached as shown in the diagram.

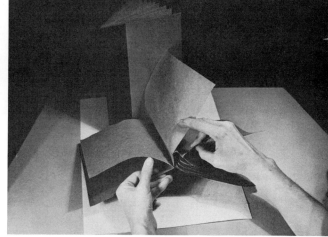

A fold of paper is inserted and glued inside each accordion pleat.

This photo shows the folds before a chipboard cover is added. A strip of cloth binds the back.

LIBRARY STYLE BINDING ON TAPES

Books on tapes permit any thickness of pages because pages are grouped together into signatures and, in the process, sewed to tapes to form reinforced bindings. Books such as these can be opened flat.

Cut sheets of paper twice the size you wish, and fold them in half. Use groups of four, one inside the other, to form a signature. Crease each fold with the back of your fingernail or a bone folder. Stack the signatures, back squared. With a pencil, mark the width of three (or more) tapes. Each mark will become the point of sewing. (Bookbinders use a sewing frame that suspends the tapes and facilitates the attachment. But it can be done without the sewing frame if you align the signatures accurately.) One signature is sewed at a time with a single linen thread through the paper and around the tapes. Pass the middle from the outside to the inside section at the pencil mark, in one, and out on the other side of the tape, across the front of the tape on the outside of the tape. Make certain that the thread does not go through the tape itself. Then open the second section at the middle and place it on top of the first signature with the fold in the same direction. Continue sewing as before—in and out and around the tapes. Draw the thread firmly but not too tightly. Place the third section in position and continue the same sewing procedure but this time making a kettle stitch to tie the third section to the one below. Continue sewing and looping the thread through the preceding signature's thread. Follow the step-by-step illustrations for binding the book.

A signature is made by folding a page in four parts. Two of these units can be combined into one signature by placing one unit into another.

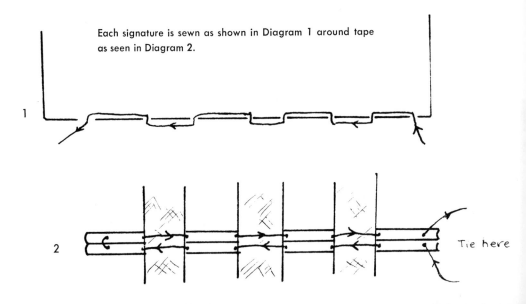

Each signature is sewn as shown in Diagram 1 around tape as seen in Diagram 2.

1

2

Tie here

The inside of each signature looks like this.

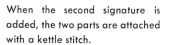

When the second signature is added, the two parts are attached with a kettle stitch.

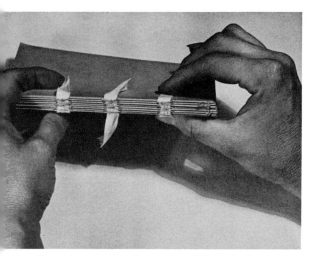

Three signatures can be connected with a kettle stitch, as well, for greater support.

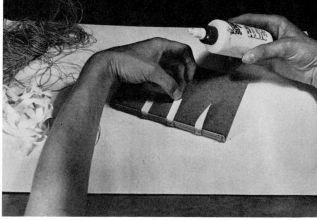

Tapes are attached to the outside of a piece of chipboard with white glue.

White glue such as Sobo (it is slightly flexible when dry) should be used along the back edge. Make certain that the signatures are square—or evenly rounded, if that is what you want.

Paint glue on the outsides of the chipboard covers . . .

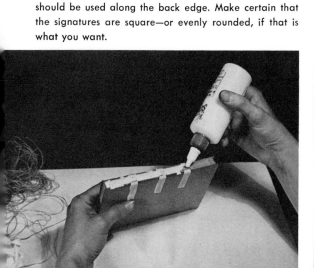

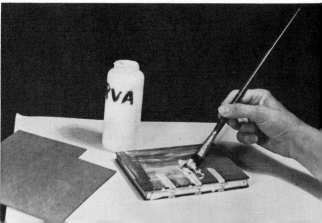

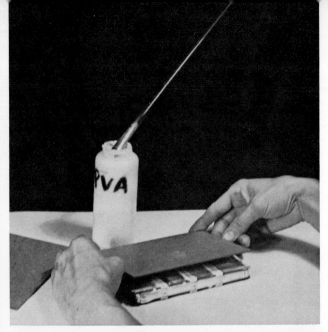

. . . and attach another piece of chipboard exactly the same size. This is an optional step. It makes for a thicker cover and seals the tapes.

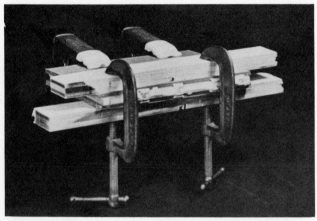

Using two strips of wood and clamps, clamp the book and allow the glue on the cover and back to dry.

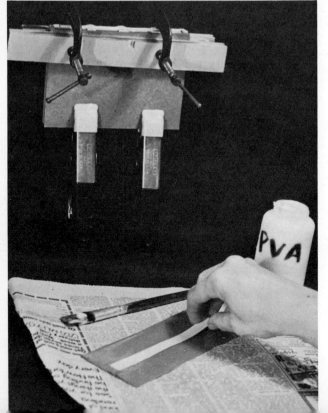

Meanwhile cut the backing from cloth, leather, or the like and add a reinforcing strip of oaktag or Scorasculpture to hold the back edge rigid when mounted and to hide the stitching.

Wrap the top edges downward and adhere the sides to the back edge of the chipboard covers.

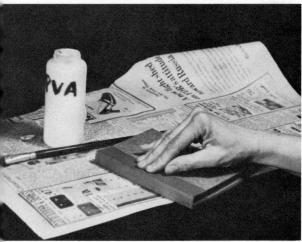

Wrap the bottom edges around the cover, even if you have to slit a signature page to do it.

Attach the decorative paper with rubber cement.

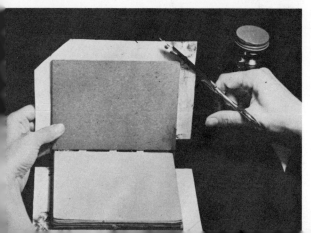

The paper should overhang to allow for the thickness of the cover, and it should overlap on three sides. Trim the corners to eliminate overlapping except at the corner tip where the paper has to cover the chipboard.

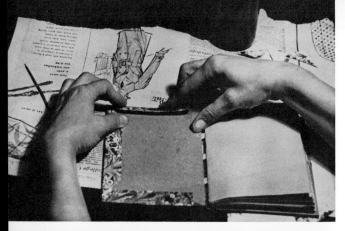

Fold the decorative paper around the cover, and glue the two opposite edges.

Pinch the corners down to cover the points, and glue the top edge to the board. Rub the entire glued area to eliminate air bubbles.

Attach the top signature page to the inside covers. This hides the tapes.

Then add a flyleaf by gluing one half of the inside cover over the first signature page that was just adhered. Trim the edge if necessary.

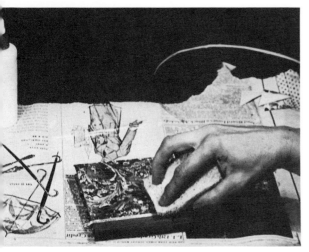

A strip of embossed foil was added as a trim. Excess white glue was sponged away with a damp sponge.

The cover was waxed.

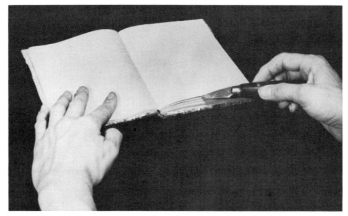

And signatures were cut. If you use a half fold, this step will not be necessary.

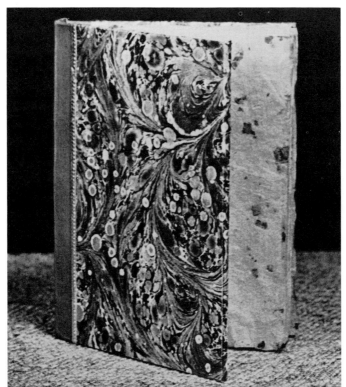

Our beautiful book.

chapter 9

Useful
and
Decorative
Forms

Useful and decorative forms made with papers are innumerable. Flowers, paintings, hats, rugs, aprons, kites, bowls, sculpture, furniture, boxes, lamps, toys, and buildings are but a few examples. In fact, there are very few ideas and products to which paper materials have not been applied. We begin this chapter with designs and techniques for making paper flowers, permanent papers, honeycombed paper forms, paper bowls, and weaving with paper twine, and we end with a Gallery of Designs showing paper's potential through what artists and designers have developed.

Concepts used throughout this book find practical application in the "Gallery." And as you will see, design potential has few limits

because of the tremendous range of processes, types of papers, and applications. The greatest innovations have broken through when the mind was not fixed with set ideas and prejudices of what paper could or could not do.

Crepe Paper Flowers

The beauty of crepe paper flowers lies not so much in the designer's ability to duplicate nature exactly as in his talent for imaginatively adding to and exaggerating the flower's design and character.

The transposition of a flower's essential character into paper can yield blossoms which will stay fresh and bright for many years. The caricaturing process is particularly enjoyable. Smoothly belled and gently fluted petals, a spreading undergrowth of green leaves, bright colors—crepe paper adopts these subtleties with just a little cutting, pulling, twisting, wiring, and gluing.

BASIC CREPE PAPER TECHNIQUES

Cutting. Crepe paper has a very definite grain, and it is along this grain that crepe paper is spread, belled, and twisted. Crepe is usually packaged with the grain lines running the width of the paper, parallel to the manufacturer's folds. To cut across the grain, then, means to cut across the fold of the crepe parallel to the end. In the diagrams that follow, the direction of the grain is indicated by parallel lines.

The fact that the manufacturer prefolds crepe paper is a distinct advantage for the flower maker. The width of most petals you will make will not exceed the length between the folds. Since many forms must be cut many times to the same pattern, by cutting through the folded sheet you will save time. The folds help in fringing as well. Fringe the folded sheet, and when it is unfolded, the entire length will be fringed.

Cupping and fluting. By cupping, petals will assume a flowerlike bell. To cup crepe paper, stretch the paper against the grain between thumb and forefinger. Flute the edge of the petal the same way, adding only a slight twist. Observe the limitations of the material; if a petal is shaped or fluted too much it will lose its grain and become droopy.

Curling. Drawing petals over the back edge of a scissors will give the paper a gentle or tight curl, depending upon how tautly the crepe paper is pulled. It is a wise idea to curl forms gradually by drawing them over the blunt edge gently several times.

Covering wire and adding leaves. Where the petals are gathered around the wire stem, cover the joint with a thin strip of green crepe paper. Wrap it around the base of the flower several times and twist it smoothly a few inches down the stem. Glue the paper in place. Leaves can be added to the stem by wrapping the leaf wire to the stem wire with a strip of crepe paper. In some cases, you may want to cover the entire stem with crepe paper. Keep the paper stretched so that the stem will be smooth.

Wiring petals and leaves. Petals and leaves can be stiffened and formed by gluing short pieces of wire to their undersides. When the glue is dry you will be able to bend the wire and thereby shape the paper. By pressing the wires into the leaves more you will also achieve an interesting veined effect.

Glues and additional materials. The best glues for flower making are the white glues and rubber cement. Be careful not to use too much of the white glues because, if they saturate the crepe paper, it may stain and become messy. Since the major joint is the point at which the paper is attached to the stem, you may want to strengthen it by wrapping with thin wire. Cover the area with a strip of crepe paper as mentioned above.

Paper flowers may be made permanent with polyester resin, which is shown later in this chapter, or they may be waterproofed and preserved by dipping them in melted wax. Allow excess wax to drip off the petals.

Special effects are possible with sprays and special crepe papers. A recommended paper is Dennison Manufacturing Co.'s Duplex. This is a two-ply paper with analogous colors on each side.

POMPON FLOWERS

This simple, pretty flower resembles no particular bloom, but a bunch of them makes a very bright, cheery bouquet.

Cut a piece of crepe paper about five inches wide across the grain, but do not unfold it. Fringe both ends deeply; the cuts should almost meet at the center, but do not cut the paper apart. After cutting, begin to unroll the fringed paper, and gather it at the same time. Tie the gathered paper at its center with a long wire stem, and fluff out the fringe to make a prickly sphere. The pompon should fill out evenly.

Add leaves, and arrange your creations to lend a perky touch to any room.

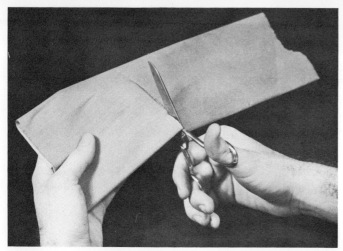

Cut a 5″ strip of crepe paper across the grain.

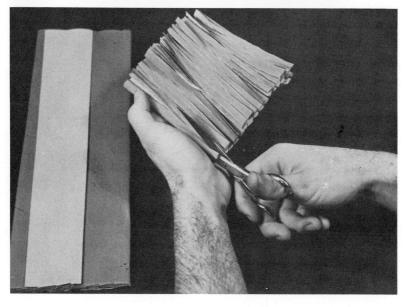

Fringe this strip from both ends. The fringes should reach almost to the center.

Unravel the fringed strip, gathering the fringes at the center. Try to gather the fringes evenly.

When you have gathered all the fringe, twist the end of a piece of florist's wire (which will serve as a stem) around the center of the fringed paper.

Gently, but firmly, tug the fringes so that they evenly fill in a sphere.

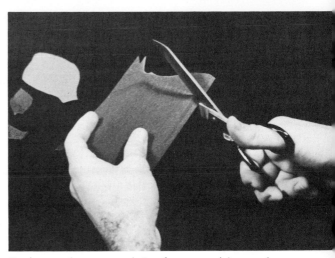

Cut leaves of your own design from several layers of green crepe paper.

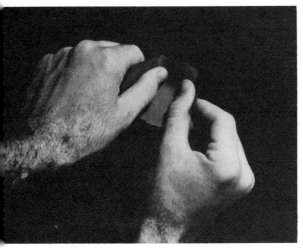

Shape the leaves as much or as little as you want.

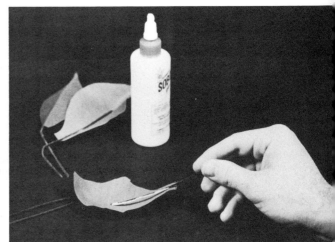

Attach wires to the undersides of the leaves. When the glue dries, bend the wires to shape the leaves.

Join the leaves to the pompons by intertwining their wires and covering the juncture with a strip of crepe paper or florist's tape. Arrange the flowers and enjoy the fringe benefits.

ORIENTAL POPPY

These flowers each require six petals of the shape shown in the diagram. Lightly flute the tops of each petal, and cup them halfway down so that they assume a gentle curve. The bright orange face of the Duplex crepe paper should be on the inside, and the amber face should be the underside of the flower.

The center of this flower is a wad of newspaper or Styrofoam covered tightly with green crepe paper. Stretch the paper over this form and crisscross the ball with a wire stem. If you are using Styrofoam you may want to use green yarn to crisscross this form and stick the wire into the ball from underneath.

Next, wrap a 1″ fringe of a dark color of crepe paper cut across the grain around the ball. Wrap it around several times, and glue the fringe down to keep it in position. This will form a feathery eyelash and make an attractive center for the flower.

Attach the petals to this center and the stem with rubber cement. Overlap them slightly. The first three petals should encircle the flower, and the next three will fill in the form. For a natural effect, make some flowers more closed than others, with one or two almost completely open.

Cover the base of the flower with a strip of crepe paper. You may want to cover the whole stem. Leaves, which can be made according to the accompanying pattern, may be attached to the flower stems or be made with stems of their own.

Cut six petals in this shape (3½″ × 3½″) out of orange/amber Duplex crepe paper. The three parallel lines indicate the direction of the grain.

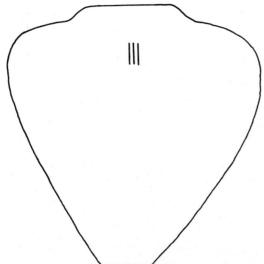

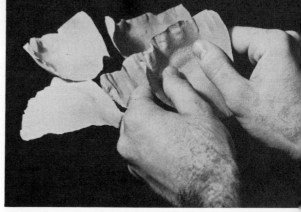

Flute the top edge, and cup the center of each petal.

To make a center around which to group the petals, cover a small ball of styrofoam (1″ in diameter) or a piece of crumpled newspaper with green crepe paper stretched tautly over its surface.

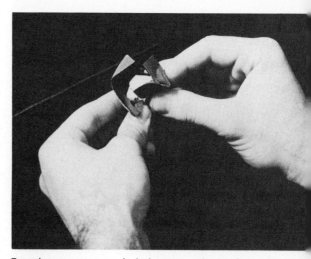

Either crisscross the wrapped ball with yarn or wrap it with the wire which will become the stem.

Cut a strip of 1" wide dark crepe paper across the grain and fringe it finely ¾" deep along one edge. Wrap and glue the strip around the base of the covered ball to form a feathery fringe for the center of the flower.

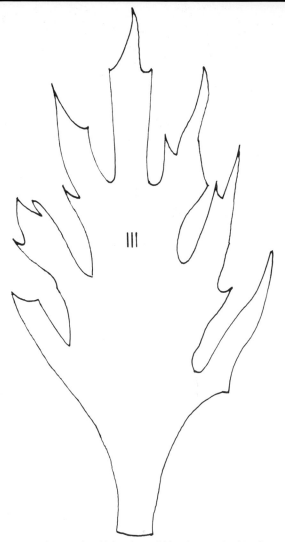

Poppy leaves should be shaped like the one in this diagram (7" long × 4" wide). The three lines indicate grain. Because of their size these leaves should be wired for support. Courtesy: Dennison Manufacturing Company.

Glue the bases of three petals to the center. Allow the petals to overlap slightly. Then attach the remaining three petals; overlap the first row. Cover the base of the flower with a strip of crepe paper. This strip may wind down the entire length of the stem.

The result is a bunch of very hoppy poppies. Design by Dennison

TIGER LILY

Pompons are imaginary, oriental poppies attempt to duplicate nature, and the tiger lily is a caricature of a wild flower.

Bright colors, extra large petals and leaves, and a long wire stamen make this crepe paper tiger lily larger than life. The lily is made with six petals, but there are two types. The three center petals are broad and have rounded tips, while the three outer petals are shorter, slimmer, and pointed. Use Duplex orange, and cut the petals from the patterns shown. A single vein was made down the center of each petal, and the petals were curled lightly.

A three-lobed yellow center (which imitates the lily's own) attaches the three inner petals. The smaller petals are then added. The amount that the outer petals overlap determines the final shape of the flower. Once these petals have been attached only the stamen need be added.

Make four stamens by tightly wrapping pieces of florist's wire with yellow or orange crepe paper. One stamen should also be the stem, but the other three will be 3″ pieces of wire that will be joined at the flower's base. Carefully push the uncovered ends of the wires through the yellow center of the flower, and wrap the wires beneath the flower to fasten wires and flower together.

Touch up the flowers by curling the petals and bending the stamens slightly. The leaves should be long and thin. Cut across the grain of the crepe paper. The leaves should be 8″ to 10″ long and no more than 2″ wide. Cut them so that they come to trenchant points, and use wire to reinforce their undersides.

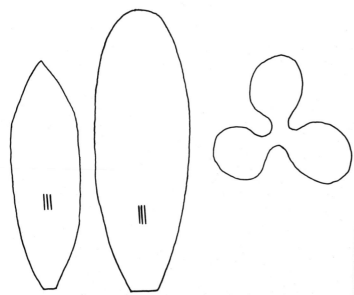

Each flower is made with three rounded petals (5″ × 1½″), three smaller pointed petals (3½″ × 1″), and a central three-lobed form (each lobe 1″ diameter).

Score each petal down its center and curl it slightly. Glue the three larger petals to the three-lobed yellow center.

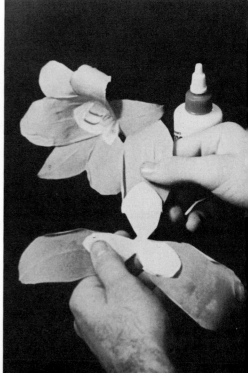

Then attach the three smaller, pointed petals at the back. The amount that the smaller petals overlap will determine the size of the flower's aperture.

The stamen is created by wrapping crepe paper around the end of the wire stem and sticking the bare end through the center of the flower. Additional stamens are shortened pieces of covered wire. Push them through the flower's center and bind the stamen wires and the crepe paper flower base with a strip of crepe paper.

An arrangement of crepe paper pompons and lilies is shown here with lily leaves. These leaves are tapered strips of green crepe supported by long single pieces of florist's wire.

These gigantic sunflowers, made in Mexico, incorporate the simple crepe paper processes of cupping and curling many petals, and fringing massive quantities of crepe. The long leaves are thin strips of green crepe which have been slitted angularly along both sides. The strips are mounted on florist's wire, and the angular fringe is then randomly bent, twisted, and ruffled. Courtesy: Fred Leighton's, New York

This crepe paper flower, also from Mexico, is made of long, broad, pointed petals which have had their lower halves gently cupped in one direction and their upper halves heavily cupped in the opposite direction. This creates the wavy, windswept effect. Courtesy: Fred Leighton's, New York

This flower was made by stretching and ruffling a long wide strip of crepe paper gathered at one end to serve as the base. It is then heavily fluted in the middle, cupped in seemingly random directions, and tightly curled along the top edge between thumb and forefinger.

A Tissue Paper Flower

Although tissue paper does not have a grain like crepe paper and cannot be shaped and stretched as easily, it does have the advantage of being sheer and delicate. Translucency and lightness make tissue paper a great material for paper flowers.

Stack six sheets of tissue paper of different colors on top of one another, placing the darkest color on the bottom and the lightest on top. Fold the sheets together into accordion pleats of about one and one-half inches. Round both ends of the pleated sheet by cutting with a scissors. Fold the folded sheets in half and wrap their center with a piece of florist's wire so that it acts as a paper clip.

Beginning with the lightest color of tissue paper (which is in the center of the flower), gently pull the tissue paper up out of the folds. Do not pull too hard or the paper will tear. Pull the petals out from both sides toward the center in a twisting motion.

Continue this process until all signs of the original pleated strip are gone and you are left with a delicate tissue paper blossom.

Pull out the individual petals from the pleats. Continue to pull the sheets of paper out to form a delicate flower.

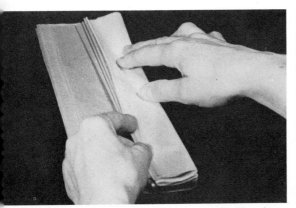

Fold six sheets of tissue paper into accordionlike pleats 1½" wide. Round the ends by cutting.

It is a handsome creation for a budding flower maker.

Fasten the center of the pleated paper tightly with a piece of florist's wire. Pass the wire around the paper by bending it over like a paper clip.

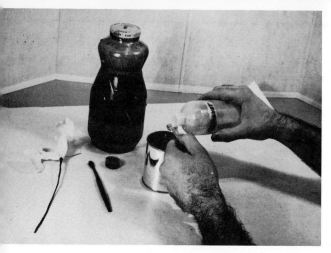

Mix the polyester resin and catalyst in a clean, uncoated metal can. Since the layer of resin will be thin, the resin should be heavily catalyzed to prevent a long sticky cure. Polyester resin and catalyst are readily available at most hardware and art stores.

Making Crepe Paper and Tissue Paper Permanent

Crepe paper and tissue paper forms may be made permanent with polyester resin. The resin is brushed on, and, when it cures, the paper will be rigidly preserved and transparent.

The only materials necessary for this process are polyester resin, catalyst, a tin can, a brush, and acetone (for cleaning the brush). The resin should be mixed with catalyst according to the instructions accompanying the polyester resin. Since only a small quantity of resin will be needed to coat most paper forms, and since the layer will be thin, the resin should be heavily catalyzed to avoid stickiness when curing.

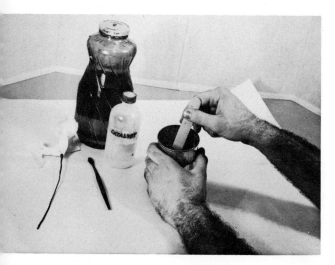

Stir the polyester resin and catalyst well.

Paint a thin coating of resin on the paper flower. Cover all surfaces. The resin will make the paper transparent.

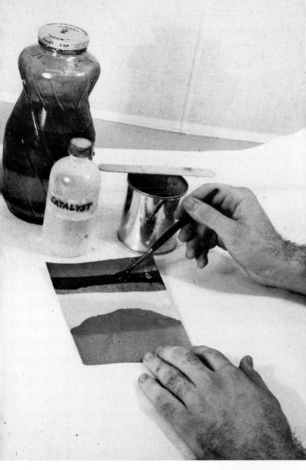

Tissue paper, and any paper product, may be preserved the same way. The polyester resin impregnates the paper fibers, stiffening, glossing, and making permanent whatever is covered with it.

The finished flower is translucent and like ceramic in texture.

Honeycombed Paper Decorations

Honeycombed paper balls, bells, flowers, circles, and parasols are familiar commercial party products, but they can also be handmade with tissue paper.

The process begins with 50 sheets of tissue paper the same size. Use different colors. The sheets are glued together with lines of glue parallel to the sheets' edges. When gluing, note particularly that glued lines alternate with each sheet. In these photographs, lighter lines indicate fresh glue that has been applied to adhere this sheet. The darker lines are glue showing through from the sheet below.

When all the sheets have been glued, allow the glue (mucilage or white) to dry fully. Make certain that the glue from previous layers does not penetrate the paper, or you may not be able to open the form. After drying, use more glue to add a piece of cardboard on each side of the stack of papers. Staple the back edge, and trim away excess tissue paper. The form is now ready to be opened and enjoyed.

Applying glue from a container like this makes the process easier. The lighter lines are where fresh glue has been applied. Be certain that you alternate lines with each sheet—if you do not, the form will not open. Also, use a glue that does not penetrate the tissue paper, or else the form will become a mass of glued paper: unopenable.

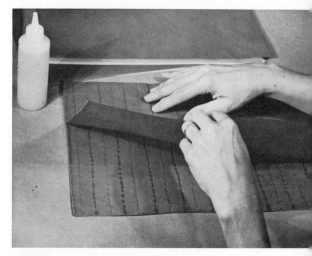

Align the next sheet and press it down so that the glue sticks to the tissue paper.

After all the sheets have been glued, allow the paper to dry fully. Then cut two semicircles or other forms and glue them to both sides of the stack of paper.

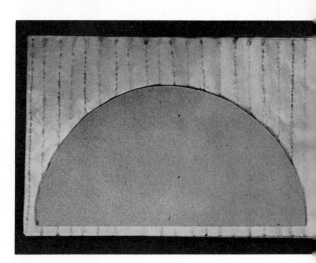

Staple the back edge of the tissue paper stack.

Trim away excess, but leave a margin of tissue paper.

The completed paper ball is a basic shape. Variations on the theme are possible by varying the contour.

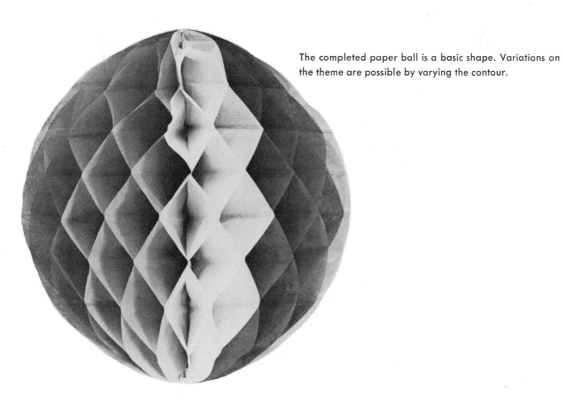

These five honeycombed paper forms are all commercial. They can all be made by hand as well, using the concepts described here, and with variations in shape.

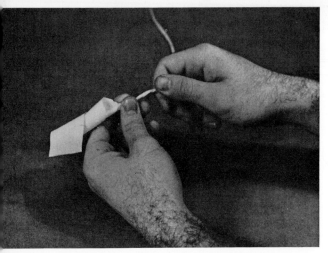

Paper twine is made by tightly twisting long strips of paper. Combine strips with a white glue.

Weaving, Knitting, and Macramé with Paper Twine

Paper twines can be used just like any other cord or yarn. You can make paper ropes easily, or buy them in a variety of thicknesses and qualities.

To make paper twine, tightly twist long strips of paper with your fingers. Use a white glue to adhere strips together for longer pieces. You will find that stiffer papers will lend themselves to twisting better than very soft ones, because when stiff ones are creased and twisted they tend to keep that shape better.

Paper twines can be adapted to most techniques requiring knotting and weaving. Macramé is especially feasible, as are large pattern weavings. The Gallery of Designs at the end of this chapter includes a very fine knitted panel made with paper twine by Mary Walker Phillips.

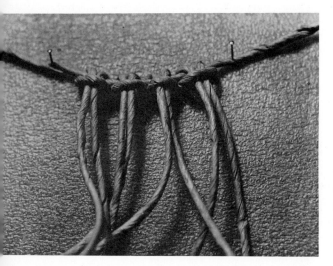

The clove hitch, a macramé beginning, is made by tying two loops over the horizontal anchor cord. Four hitches, each made with a separate, long piece of cord, are shown here.

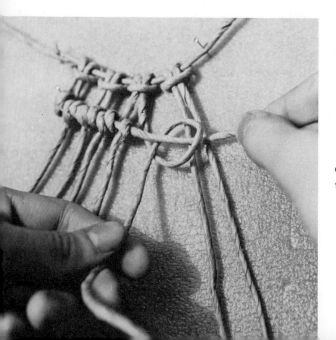

One variation of knotting is the horizontal clove hitch tied in series like this.

264

The finished necklace shows the use of both horizontal and diagonal clove hitches. The ends of the paper twine were unwound to produce a fringe effect. Paper twine can be used in a variety of macramé patterns and for a host of purposes.

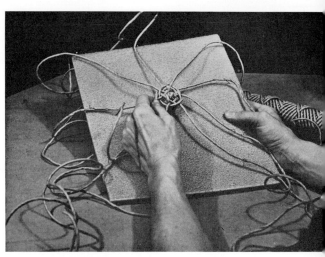

Four crosspieces of paper twine and a single length were crossed to create nine spokes in this weaving. Another piece of twine, tied at the center, is woven around these spokes.

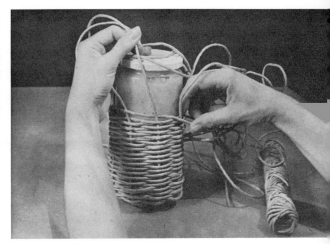

Once the bottom has been woven, a bottle is inserted to hold and help mold the shape of the weaving. A roll of paper twine is visible at the right.

Every other spoke-cord is turned back into the weaving when the form is high enough. These spokes are woven back and knotted for decorative purposes.

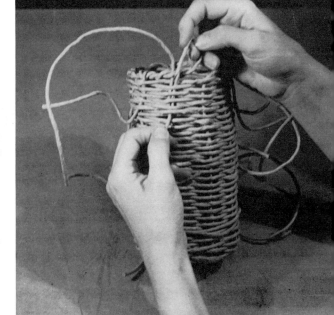

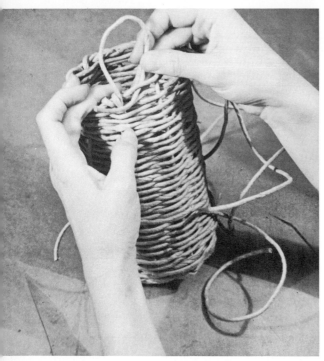

Other spoke-cords are looped around the top layer of cord several times. These will act as hanging cords later.

The finished weaving will be a good insulator for your favorite beverage

This marvelous hat was knitted by Mary Walker Phillips with paper twine. Courtesy: Mary Walker Phillips, photograph by Ferdinand Boesch

Artape is wrapped around a piece of florist's wire to form a paper bead.

Paper Beads

Paper beads can be made by winding any paper, but gummed papers like Artape have a decided advantage. The easiest, most uniform bead to make is rolled from an elongated isosceles triangle of paper. The longer the paper the more gradually and evenly the bead will taper.

Other forms can be made by cutting strips of paper in uneven shapes and rolling them. Try to roll the papers over a thin piece of wire that will slide out from the center of the bead easily. The wire leaves a hole to enable you to string the beads.

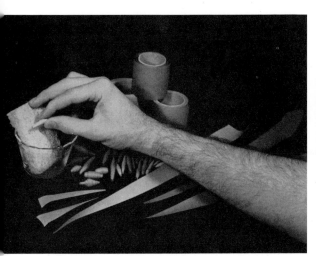

Slide the wire out of the bead, wet the gummed back of the Artape, and close the bead by pasting down the end.

These beads were strung on nylon string.

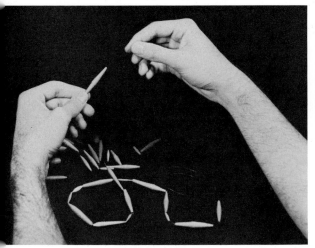

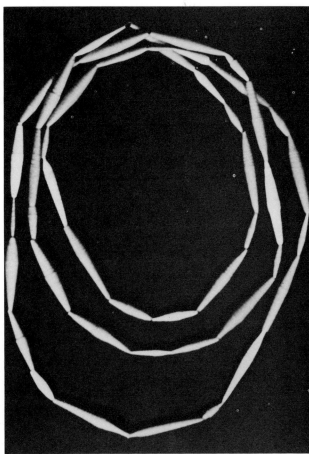

Finished necklace of paper beads in analogous colors of reds and violets in varying sizes.

Paper quilling (called Cerami and Pottery Paper) comes in a variety of sizes. It is actually just a very long strip of paper wound tightly, much like a roll of brown gummed paper (without the glue).

Paper Quilling

Tightly wound strips of paper, paper quilling, can be pressed into a variety of shapes and made permanent to create attractive sculpture and decorations. This material is readily available under the generic name of paper quilling and is sold by American Handicrafts under the trade name of Cerami Paper, and by the Labelon Corporation under the name of Pottery Paper.

These rolls of paper come in different sizes. The quilling should be shaped carefully, because if the roll is extended too far it will come apart—and cannot be put back together again. To shape this material, apply even pressure between thumb and forefingers. Practice shaping the quilling—it can be pressed back into a flat roll, but this, too, should be done slowly and carefully.

The rolls can also be shaped over other forms such as bowls, glasses, and jars. It takes contours very well.

When you have decided on a shape you want to preserve, paint the inside with an acrylic medium, white glue, or plastic glaze. The form may be painted with acrylic paints.

Epoxy resin is another method of making paper quilling permanent. Two-part epoxy cements are available at all hardware and art supply stores. Simply mix the two parts and apply a thin layer to the paper. If the epoxy is clear, the paper will become darker (since the paper absorbs the resin). When the epoxy cures. the form will be exceptionally strong and permanent.

Shape the paper by applying even, careful pressure between thumb and forefinger. Be careful! If you force one area out too far, the roll will come apart, and it is impossible to put back together again.

Quilling can result in very smooth, gradual forms like this one if the pressure is applied evenly.

When you have achieved the desired shape, use an acrylic medium, white glue, epoxy, or plastic glaze to make it permanent. Paint both the inside and outside.

This form was painted with an acrylic paint, and is now being decorated with cord adhered with a plastic glaze.

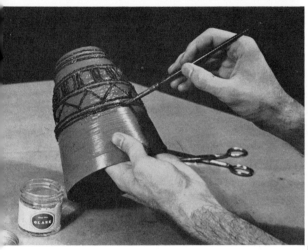

You can apply different kinds of decorations to this material.

The finished glazed container.

This bowl is made permanent with a polymer medium.

The next step is the mixing of epoxy cement.

The epoxy, being applied to the bowl's cover, darkens the paper because it is being absorbed. This technique is the most permanent way of preserving paper.

The epoxy interior is almost indestructible.

This bowl is a very strong, permanent form.

Here a number of smaller forms in paper quilling are being strung on a piece of wire to create a sculpture.

Sobo glue is used to adhere the different parts.

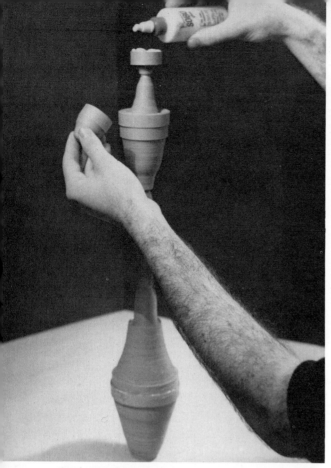

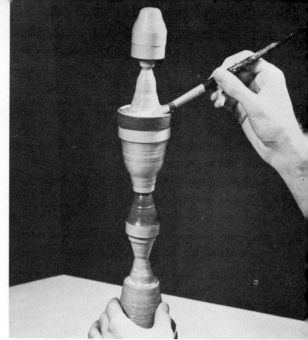

Different areas are then decorated with Liquitex's Modular Acrylic Colors.

Stack and glue unit over unit.

The whole sculpture is then coated with a plastic glaze, Mod Podge, or polyvinyl acetate.

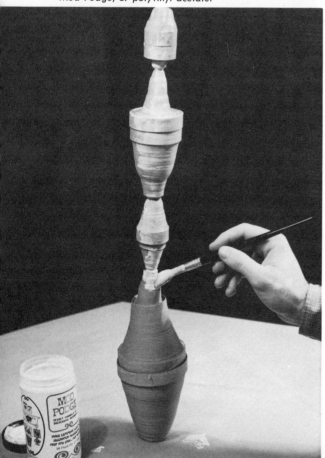

This tower looks tipsy because it lost the mooring at one of its joints.

Paper Boxes

Paper boxes are probably the most common of all paper products. Almost everything comes in a paper box: clothes, food, mail, books, film, tools, appliances—even paper. Most boxes are constructed very simply using tabs and gluing or taping the bottoms and tops with paper tape. Craftsmen can make those boxes, and more interesting ones as well. It is intriguing to take apart various cardboard boxes to study their construction. There are a great many ways to cut a box shape economically from a single piece of paper.

Another basic box form.

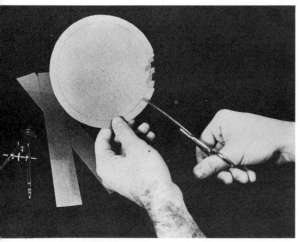

A round paper box can be constructed from two pieces of paper. The bottom is a circle. Cut out the circle, and mark another circle within this one approximately ½″ from the outer edge. Fringe this outer circle as shown.

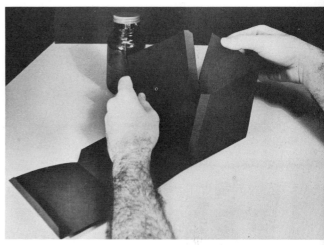

The tabs are glued to the box walls with rubber cement.

A strip of paper long enough to reach around the bottom circle is attached to the tabs with rubber cement.

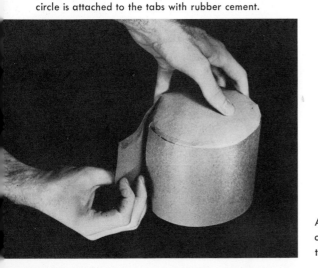

A scored paper ornament decorates this box.

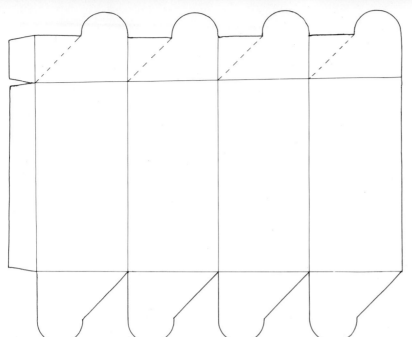

This diagram is for a more sophisticated box. The dotted lines represent score lines on one side; the solid lines indicate scoring on the other side.

Attach the tabs so that a rectangular shape is formed, and fold down the tops as shown here. The size of this box can be varied.

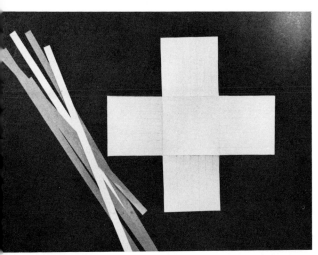

The diagram shown here is for a box-basket. The strips of paper on the left are woven to give the box form.

Cut through the paper along the indicated lines. But cut only to within ½" of the top in each of the four sections.

Weave the paper strips through the slits that you have cut.

The handle for this basket is a chain of paper strips. Each paper link was folded in half, and then each half was folded in half again toward the center . . .

. . . the next link was then passed through the loops of the preceding one.

The round box and woven basket.

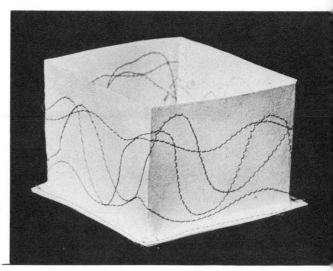

A unique box of Acta, a blotterlike mat textured paper, was decorated on a sewing machine, and then the sides were sewn to the base.

This box is manufactured of die-cut paperboard. Courtesy: Société Bremo

Portuguese cardboard boxes covered with embroidered cotton. Courtesy: Brimful House

These boxes collapse when the piece of board hinged at their bottoms is pushed up.

Four paper boxes were combined in this chest of drawers (3″ × 3″ × 3″). The base is chipboard, and the covering is glazed paper.

The "Quadralon" is a special packaging designed by Jim Hanko for the Weyerhaeuser Co. Courtesy: The Weyerhaeuser Co.

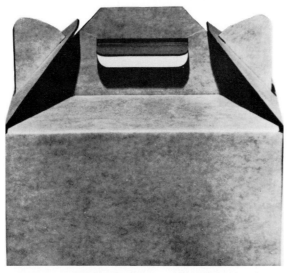

A pet carrier of solid fiberboard manufactured by the Container Corporation of America. Courtesy: Container Corporation of America

Even Coca-Cola comes in paper boxes. Courtesy: Container Corporation of America

Paper Lampshades

Many commercial lampshades are made of scored and folded papers. Others are made in a pleated design. Some examples are shown in the Gallery of Designs that follows. The one illustrated here is an attractive form constructed with a few simple scores and folds. The geometry of paper sculpture finds direct application here.

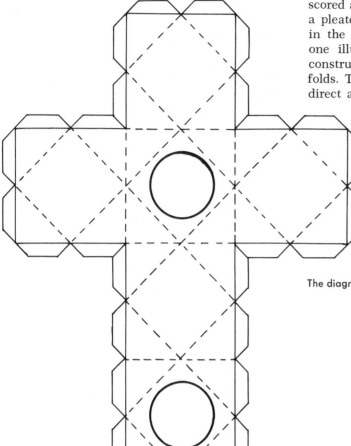

The diagram is for a paper lampshade.

Score on the indicated lines and attach the tabs with rubber cement.

The finished lampshade is quite attractive.

A Gallery of Designs in Paper

Paper surrounds us, but, as with any material, good design is not a plentiful commodity. This section contains a collection of exciting, well-designed, practical, and useful forms constructed with paper materials. Paper depicted here, surprisingly, is used where permanence is a criterion, in furniture, rugs, clothing accessories, lampshades, and, paradoxically, where paper fulfills a temporary need such as in decorations for special occasions. These designs demonstrate clearly the tremendous range of possibilities in using paper; its plasticity is evident, but, more important, it has an integrated and ubiquitous place in our lives.

H. L. Goodspeed's puzzle of seven pieces of connected cubes made of scored and folded paperboard is an intriguing paper toy. Courtesy: Container Corporation of America and The Museum of Contemporary Crafts

A folded paper hat in gay colors and patterns is intended for beach and sunny weather wear. Courtesy: Bonnie Cashin Designs.

Bonnie Cashin's tufted paper coat is perfect insulation for snow country. Courtesy: Bonnie Cashin Designs

Indian *dugdugi* clay drums have paper heads. Courtesy: Brimful House

Russian toy accordions use a paper bellows. Courtesy: Brimful House

This horse, made of paper glued to a bamboo frame, is used in Indian religious processions (57" high). Courtesy: Container Corporation of America and The Museum of Contemporary Crafts

This 20th century Japanese fan is constructed of paper and wood. Courtesy: Metropolitan Museum of Art

A Chinese fan of the Ch'ien Period (1736–95) made of ivory, paper, and bamboo. Courtesy: Metropolitan Museum of Art, Gift of Mr. B. I. Kinne

Jewel in the Grass (2' × 3') by Nell Znamierowski is a weaving of rya knots around a paper warp with the addition of washers and solder cores. It is in the collection of the Art Institute of Chicago. Courtesy: Nell Znamierowski, Photograph by Ferdinand Boesch

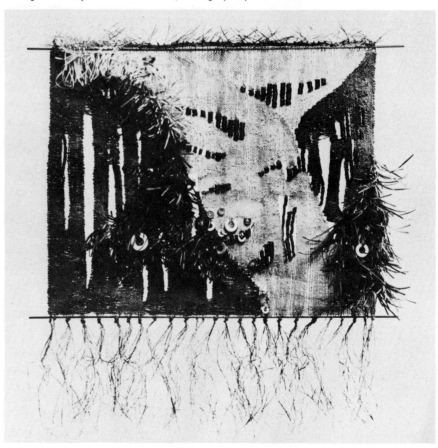

Mary Walker Phillips designed and knitted this exciting form from paper string. Courtesy: Mary Walker Phillips, Photograph by Ferdinand Boesch

White Peacock (20″ × 40″), also by Nell Znamierowski, is woven of paper and plastic yarns. The warp is 100% paper. Courtesy: Nell Znamierowski

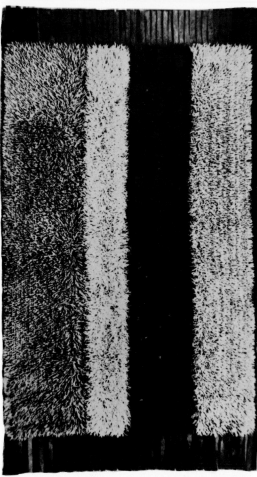

The "Seascape" rug of tufted paper yarn on latex backing was designed for Regal Rugs by Elenhank Designers. Courtesy: Regal Rugs, Inc.

This rug from Regal's experimental collection is designed to be disposable. Courtesy: Regal Rugs, Inc.

A "Bird's Nest" rug, 54" diameter, of tufted and quilted paper is also priced to toss away. Courtesy: Regal Rugs, Inc.

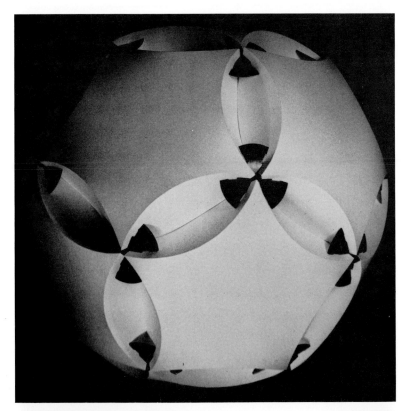

This marvelous "Facet" lamp is made entirely of scored and folded circles of paper attached with smaller circles, by Cardboard Engineering, Ltd.

An opaque paper is cut out and a translucent paper is pasted inside this Indian lamp so that it will glow from within. The translucent paper is painted in transparent colors.

This classic Japanese lamp is made of paper over bamboo strips.

A lampshade of cut, scored, and folded paper by Staples and Gray of England. Courtesy: Container Corporation of America and The Museum of Contemporary Crafts

Another Japanese lamp with a paper cylinder to diffuse light. The bamboo frame is on the outside to protect the inner tube of light.

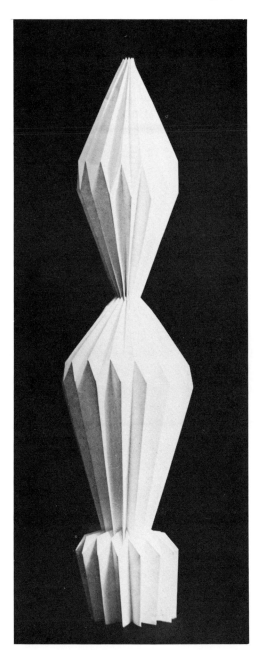

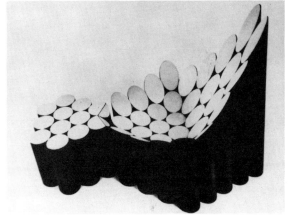

Donald Lloyd McKinley glued and riveted cardboard tubes to construct this chair and ottoman (45″ × 64″ × 34½″). Courtesy: Donald Lloyd McKinley

Pleated and folded papers have long been a favorite of lighting designers.

These children's chairs of wire-reinforced fiberboard are manufactured by the Container Corporation of America. Courtesy: Container Corporation of America

Stool (12″ high × 17″ diameter) and chair (31″ high × 18″ diameter) are made of compressed paper tube, designed by Jean-Louis Avril. Courtesy: Container Corporation of America and The Museum of Contemporary Crafts

Kano Sanraku (1559–1635) painted this eight-fold screen of birds and millet with color and gold leaf on paper. Courtesy: Metropolitan Museum of Art

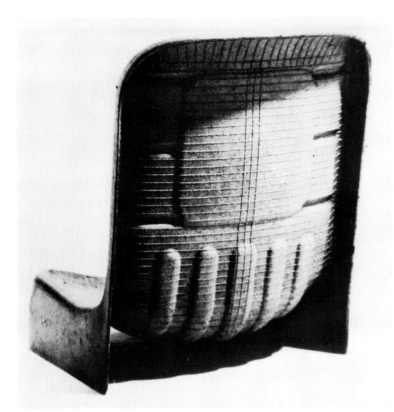

This automobile seat of pressure-molded "Prestfiber" is manufactured by British Moulded Fibre for the British Motor Corporation. Courtesy: Container Corporation of America and The Museum of Contemporary Crafts

In a beautiful blending of design and function, chaise longue and ottoman, from the "Easy Edges" collection designed by architect Frank O. Gehry, curve together as a unit or can be used separately. The revolutionary new material is "Edgeboard Sections," made of cross-laminated layers of corrugated fiberboard. Cantilevered construction and the remarkable resilient quality of the material with its suedelike surface provide relaxing comfort. Courtesy: Kairalla Agency, Photograph by Pat Faure

Fantasy bar and stool, from the "Easy Edges" collection designed by Frank O. Gehry. In addition to its use as a bar, this combination also makes a great desk—it's a perfect height for typing—and a comfortable perch for reading. Courtesy: Kairalla Agency, Photograph by Pat Faure

appendix

Chronological History of Paper

2200 B.C.	Papyrus manuscript
250 B.C.	Chinese Mêng T'ien invents the camel's hair brush
A.D. 105	Ts'ai Lun invents paper made from mulberry and other bark, fish-nets, hemp, and rags
106	use of spirit money made of paper
400	invention of true ink in China
500	the Mayans invent bark paper
610	papermaking is introduced into Japan from China
650–83	Chinese invent paper money in the T'ang Dynasty of Emperor Kao Tsung
751	Chinese prisoners of war teach papermaking secrets to Turks in Samarkand
868	earliest printed book, the *Diamond Sutra,* by Wang Chieh, is found in Tun-huang
950	earliest use of paper in Spain
969	earliest record of playing cards in China
1041–49	invention of movable type in China by Pi Shêng, movable type better for other languages using a simpler alphabet form
1116	Chinese make the first stitched books
1276	first mention of the Fabriano paper mill in Italy
1309	first use of paper in England
1400	paper has replaced parchment in Europe to a great extent
1423	beginning of block printing in Europe using an ancient Chinese technique for making playing cards
1549	Spanish missionary Diego de Landa burns the library of the Mayas
1575–80	first paper mill is established in Culhuacán
1690	first paper mill in North America, near Germantown, Pa.
1719	René de Réaumur, noticing wasps using wood fibers for making their nests, writes about the possibility of using wood
1798	papermaking machine is invented by a Frenchman, Nicholas-Louis Robert

294

1806   Henry and Sealy Fourdrinier patent improvements in Robert's machine

1817   the first paper machine in America, Thomas Gilpin's near Philadephia

1827   the first Fourdrinier machine is erected at Saugerties, New York

1841   Charles Fenerty, of Nova Scotia, produces the first ground wood paper in the Western Hemisphere

1844   first commercial paper boxes are produced by Col. Andrew Dennison in Brunswick, Maine, beginning of Dennison Mfg. Co.

1850   first paper bags made by hand, and a German, Friedrich Gottlob Keller, writes of a machine to grind wood into fibers

1855   wrappings and fibers of Egyptian mummies are imported to make paper

1856   corrugated paper is patented in England

1865   Benjamin Tilghman, an American, discovers sulfite process for dissolving resins in wood

1868   paper is used for the following: boxes, cups, plates, washbowls, barrels, tabletops, roofing, shades, collars, vests, cuffs, aprons, towels, napkins, buttons, hats, handkerchiefs, raincoats, corsets, slippers, slips, curtains, carpets, machine belts, wrappings of various kinds, etc.

1878   paper dome for observatory of Rensselaer Polytechnic Institute, Troy, N.Y.

1906   first paper milk cartons are made by G. W. Maxwell, San Francisco, Calif.

1945   there are 14,000 different paper products

1971   net sales in the U.S. for paper and allied products equal $22,224,-000,000; paper and paperboard account for $54,428,000; 230 million books are printed in the U.S., and each person in the U.S. uses 569 pounds of paper

bibliography

ARTES DE MEXICO, Mexico City, Mexico, #124 and 1970–71 Annual.

ASPDEN, GEORGE. *Model Making in Paper and Cardboard*. New York: Reinhold Publishing Corporation, 1964.

BRUMMITT, WYATT. *Kites*. New York: Golden Press Western Publishing Co., Inc., 1971.

CHRISTENSEN, BODI, and MARTI, SAMUEL. *Witchcraft and Pre-Columbian Paper*. Mexico City: Ediciones Euroamericanas, 1971.

Combed Pattern Papers. Northgates, Leicester: The Dryad Press.

GARRETT, LILLIAN. *Visual Design*. New York: Reinhold Publishing Corporation, 1967.

GRATER, MICHAEL. *Paper Faces*. New York: Taplinger Publishing Co., Inc., 1968.

————. *Paper People*. New York: Taplinger Publishing Co., Inc., 1970.

HEWITT-BATES, J. S., and HALLIDAY, J. *Three Methods of Marbling*. Northgates, Leicester: The Dryad Press.

HOLLANDER, ANNETTE. *Decorative Papers and Fabrics*. New York: Van Nostrand Reinhold Co., 1971.

HONDA, ISAO. *Mon-Kiri*. Tokyo: Japan Publications Trading Co., Ltd., 1959.

————, ed. *Origami*. Tokyo: Toto Shuppan Co., Ltd., 1957.

HUGHES, TONI. *How to Make Shapes in Space*. New York: E. P. Dutton & Co., Inc., 1956.

HUNTER, DARD. *Papermaking*. New York: Alfred A. Knopf, 1967.

JOHNSTON, MARY GRACE. *Paper Shapes and Sculpture*. Worcester, Mass.: Davis Publications, Inc., 1958.

JOHNSTON, MEDA PARKER, and KAUFMAN, GLEN. *Design on Fabrics*. New York: Van Nostrand Reinhold Co., 1967.

KENNY, CARLA and JOHN B. *Design in Papier-Mâché.* Philadelphia: Chilton Book Company, 1971.

KEPES, GYORGY. *Language of Vision.* Chicago: Paul Theobald, 1944.

LEWIS, A.W. *Basic Bookbinding.* New York: Dover Publications, Inc., 1957.

Made with Paper, an exhibition in 1970 at the Museum of Contemporary Crafts, New York.

MAILE, ANNE. *Tie and Dye.* New York: Ballantine Books, 1971.

MEILACH, DONA Z. *Macramé Accessories.* New York: Crown Publishers, Inc., 1972.

————. *Macramé: Creative Design in Knotting.* New York: Crown Publishers, Inc., 1971.

————. *Papier-Mâché Artistry.* New York: Crown Publishers, Inc., 1971.

MOHOLY-NAGY, L. *Vision in Motion.* Chicago: Paul Theobald, 1947.

MOOREY, ANNE and CHRISTOPHER. *Making Mobiles.* New York: Watson-Guptill, 1966.

MOSELEY, SPENCER; JOHNSON, PAULINE; and KOENIG, HAZEL. *Craft Design.* Belmont, Calif.: Wadsworth Publishing Co., Inc., 1963.

MUNSON, DON, and ROSSE, ALLIANORA. *The Paper Book.* New York: Charles Scribner's Sons, 1970.

NEWMAN, JAY HARTLEY and LEE SCOTT. *Plastics for the Craftsman.* New York: Crown Publishers, Inc., 1972.

NEWMAN, THELMA R. *Contemporary Decoupage.* New York: Crown Publishers, Inc., 1972.

————. *Plastics as an Art Form.* Philadelphia: Chilton Book Company, 1969.

————. *Plastics as Design Form.* Philadelphia: Chilton Book Company, 1972.

————. *Wax as Art Form.* Cranbury, New Jersey: Thomas Yoseloff, Ltd., 1966.

OGAWA, HIROSHI. *The Art of Paper Craft.* London: B. T. Batsford, Ltd., 1971.

OGDEN, JOY. *Models in Vellum Paper.* Northgates, Leicester: The Dryad Press.

Paper and Paper Manufacture. New York: The American Paper Institute, 1972.

RAINEY, SARITA R. *Weaving Without a Loom.* Worcester, Mass.: Davis Publications, Inc., 1970.

ROTTGER, ERNST. *Creative Paper Craft.* London: B. T. Batsford, Ltd., 1970.

RUBI, CHRISTIAN. *Cut Paper Silhouettes and Stencils.* London: Kaye & Ward, 1972.

SAITO, TADAO. *High Fliers.* Tokyo: Japan Publications, Inc., 1969.

SEITZ, WILLIAM C. *The Art of Assemblage.* New York: Museum of Modern Art, 1961.

STROSE, SUZANNE. *Coloring Papers.* New York: Sterling Publishing Co., Inc., 1969.

SUTCLIFFE, THOMAS, and ROGERS, EDWARD. *Introducing Constructional Art.* New York: Watson-Guptill, 1970.

Working with Paper. New York: Franklin Watts, Inc., 1971.

YAMADA, SADAMI, and ITO, KIYOTADA. *New Dimensions in Paper Craft.* Tokyo: Japan Publications Trading Co., 1967.

supply sources

ADHESIVES

Slomons Labs, Inc.
32-45 Hunter's Point Ave.
Long Island City, N.Y. 11101
Sobo, Velverette, Quik
Stationery stores, five-and-tens, hardware stores, paint stores, arts and crafts stores

BOOKBINDING MATERIALS AND EQUIPMENT

The Craftool Co., Inc.
1 Industrial Road
Wood-Ridge, N.J. 07075

School Products Co.
312 E. 23rd St.
New York, N.Y. 10010

Talas Division of Technical Library Service
104 5th Ave.
New York, N.Y. 10011

DECOUPAGE PRINTS AND MATERIALS

Boins Arts and Crafts Co.
91 Morris St.
Morristown, N.J. 07960 and
75 South Palm Ave.,
Sarasota, Fla. 33577

Connoisseur Studios, Inc.
Louisville, Ky. 40207
Paper tole prints and decoupage supplies

Dick Blick
P.O. Box 1267
Galesburg, Ill. 61401
Arts and crafts departments and stores

DYES FOR BATIK AND DIP-DYEING

Aljo Manufacturing
116 Prince St.
New York, N.Y. 10012

298

Commercial Art Materials Co.
165 Lexington Ave.
New York, N.Y., 10016

The Craftool Co., Inc.
1 Industrial Road
Wood-Ridge, N.J. 07075

The Crystal Tissue Co.
Middletown, Ohio 45042
Dippity papers and dyes

Fibrec, Inc.
2795 16th St.
San Francisco, Calif. 94130

Gothic Color Co., Inc.
727 Washington St.
New York, N.Y. 10014

Hazel Pearsons Handicrafts
4128 Temple City Blvd.
Rosemead, Calif. 91770

GENERAL SUPPLIERS

(Papers, dyes, scissors, paper cutters, rulers, adhesives, paints, etc.)

Boins Arts and Crafts Co.
91 Morris St.
Morristown, N.J. 07960 and
75 South Palm Ave.
Sarasota, Fla. 33577

CCM: Arts and Crafts, Inc.
9520 Baltimore Ave.
College Park, Md. 20740

Dick Blick
P.O. Box 1267
Galesburg, Ill. 61401

Economy Handicrafts, Inc.
47-11 Francis Lewis Blvd.
Flushing, N.Y. 11361

J. L. Hammett Co.
Boston, Mass. 02114
Braintree, Mass. 02184
Lynchburg, Va., 24502
Lyons, N.Y. 14489
Union, N.J., 07083

NASCO
Fort Atkinson, Wis. 53538

Pyramid Paper Co.
310 S. Morgan St.
Tampa, Fla. 33602

Sax Arts and Crafts
P.O. Box 2002
Milwaukee, Wis. 53201

KITE MATERIALS

Go Fly a Kite Shop
1613 Second Ave.
New York, N.Y. 10028
Kites, bamboo, papers, cords, reels

Kyte House
Richardson, Tex. 75080
Kites and accessories

MISCELLANEOUS

DRYING PLANTS
Artis Inc.
9123 E. Las Tunas
Temple City, Calif. 91780
Flower Dri

DRY BUTTERFLIES
Dorothy Biddle Service
Hawthorne, N.Y. 10532

RUBBING KIT
Yasutomo and Company
24 California St.
San Francisco, Calif. 94111

PAINTS AND GLAZES

Activa Products, Inc.
7 Front St.
San Francisco, Calif. 94111
Activa Clear Glaze

American Crayon Co.
Sandusky, Ohio, 44870
Prang Products

Permanent Pigments
2700 Highland Ave.
Norwood
Cincinnati, Ohio, 45212
Liquitex Products

PAPER TAPE

Tape, Inc.
2612 South Broadway
Green Bay, Wis. 54305
Artape

PAPER MAKING EQUIPMENT

(molds and deckles, beaters, pulps, felt blankets)

Albany Felt Co.
1373 Broadway
Menands, N.Y. 12204

The Craftool Co., Inc.
1 Industrial Road
Wood-Ridge, N.J. 07075

PAPERS

Andrews-Nelson-Whitehead
7 Laight St.
New York, N.Y. 10013
Handmade and exotic papers

Aquabee
P.O. Box 1016-100 Eighth St.
Passaic, N.J. 07055
General selection

Bienfang Paper Co., Inc.
P.O. Box 408
Metuchen, N.J. 07840
General selection

Central Art Supply Co.
62 3rd Ave.
New York, N.Y. 10013

Charles T. Bainbridge's Sons
20 Cumberland St.
Brooklyn, N.Y. 11205

Crystal Craft Art Tissue Co.
Middletown, Ohio 45042
Tissue paper

David Davis
530 La Guardia Place
New York, N.Y.
Handmade and exotic papers

Dennison Manufacturing Co.
Framingham, Mass. 01701
Scorasculpture, crepe paper, and Duplex crepe

Joseph Torch
147 W. 14th St.
New York, N.Y., 10011

Paperchase Products, Ltd.
216 Tottenham Court Rd.
London W. 1, England
Handmade and exotic papers

Riverside Paper Corp.
Appleton, Wisconsin 54911
Dubl-hue 2-tone paper

Rupaco Paper Corp.
62 Kent St.
Brooklyn, N.Y. 11222
General selection

Technical Papers Corp.
729 Boylston St.
Boston, Mass. 02116
Tableau-block printing paper

Three Arts Materials Group, Inc.
375 Great Neck Rd.
Great Neck, N.Y. 11021
Acta sewable paper

PAPIER-MACHE

Activa Products, Inc.
7 Front St.
San Francisco, Calif. 94111
Celluclay instant papier-mâché

Riverside Paper Corp.
Appleton, Wis. 54911
Decomâché

QUILLING

Labelon Corp.
10 Chapin St.
Canandaigua, N.Y. 14424
Called Pottery Paper

American Handicrafts Co.
Tandy Corp.
P.O. Box 791
Fort Worth, Tex. 76107
Called Cerami Paper

index